Comments on other *Amazing Stories* from readers & reviewers

"Tightly written volumes filled with lots of wit and humour about famous and infamous Canadians."
Eric Shackleton, *The Globe and Mail*

"The heightened sense of drama and intrigue, combined with a good dose of human interest is what sets Amazing Stories *apart."*
Pamela Klaffke, *Calgary Herald*

"This is popular history as it should be... For this price, buy two and give one to a friend."
Terry Cook, a reader from Ottawa, on **Rebel Women**

"Glasner creates the moment of the explosion itself in graphic detail...she builds detail upon gruesome detail to create a convincingly authentic picture."
Peggy McKinnon, *The Sunday Herald*, on **The Halifax Explosion**

"It was wonderful...I found I could not put it down. I was sorry when it was completed."
Dorothy F. from Manitoba on **Marie-Anne Lagimodière**

"Stories are rich in description, and bristle with a clever, stylish realness."
Mark Weber, *Central Alberta Advisor*, on **Ghost Town Stories II**

"A compelling read. Bertin...has selected only the most intriguing tales, which she narrates with a wealth of detail."
Joyce Glasner, *New Brunswick Reader*, on **Strange Events**

"The resulting book is one readers will want to share with all the women in their lives."
Lynn Martel, *Rocky Mountain Outlook*, on **Women Explorers**

THE LAST OF
THE BEOTHUK

AMAZING STORIES®

THE LAST OF THE BEOTHUK

A Canadian Tragedy

HISTORY

by Barbara Whitby

PUBLISHED BY ALTITUDE PUBLISHING CANADA LTD.
1500 Railway Avenue, Canmore, Alberta T1W 1P6
www.altitudepublishing.com
1-800-957-6888

Extreme care has been taken to ensure that all information presented in
this book is accurate and up to date. Neither the author nor the
publisher can be held responsible for any errors.

Publisher	Stephen Hutchings
Associate Publisher	Kara Turner
Editor	Dianne Smyth

We acknowledge the financial support of the Government
of Canada through the Book Publishing Industry Development
Program (BPIDP) for our publishing activities.

Altitude GreenTree Program
Altitude Publishing will plant twice as many trees as were used
in the manufacturing of this product.

National Library of Canada Cataloguing in Publication Data

Whitby, Barbara
  Last of the Beothuk / Barbara Whitby.

(Amazing stories)
ISBN 1-55439-030-3

  1. Shanawdithit, ca. 1800-1829. 2. Beothuk Indians--Biography.
I. Title. II. Series: Amazing stories (Calgary, Alta.)

E99.B4S53 2005   971.8'004973   C2005-903552-8

Amazing Stories® is a registered trademark of Altitude Publishing Canada Ltd.

Printed and bound in Canada by Friesens
2 4 6 8 9 7 5 3 1

For my daughters Philippa and Andrea,
with much love. Thank you for supporting
me from the beginning in this adventure.

Contents

Author's Note

Racist words and attitudes have been quoted occasionally in this book to emphasize ways of thinking that were common in earlier times. Their use is intended to accurately convey the story in context as it unfolded in years past. To deliberately use the word "savage" of another human being now is most offensive and absolutely unacceptable. Passages in the book that refer to Canada's Native peoples in a derogatory manner are based on contemporary letters and documents, and in no way reflect the opinion of the author. From the earliest contact, the belief that Native peoples were sub-human was widespread, and often led to contemptuous attitudes and brutal behaviour. Although attitudes have changed considerably, it should be noted that redressing these wrongs is still in process.

Prologue

James Carey, a trapper from Twillingate thought he was alone when he first sighted some figures farther down the shore of Badger Bay. They were moving out of the shelter of the forest. He stiffened. Are they friendly? Or are they hostile "savages"?

On this cold January morning of 1823, he had reason to be uneasy. He had boasted over many a pint of ale that he always killed any "Red Indians" who strayed into his path. Thieving nuisances. He thought of them as less than human. Being quite ruthless excited him.

Squinting against the glare of the snow, he fired a warning shot over their heads. He knew from experience that if they were Red Indians, they would most likely run. These "savages" were deathly afraid of firearms. But what could a man expect? They were brutes — scarcely more than animals — and much more sport to hunt.

He was shocked when the two figures continued to advance without apparent fear. Yes, they were from the Red Indian tribe. Their clothes and faces were heavily stained with greasy red mud. When he realized they were making directly for him, he turned back, in panic, towards the cabin where his partner Stephen Adams waited.

"Adams!" *he screamed with genuine fear. "Out here!*
Indians!"

Adams raced out to join him, and they stood with their
guns lined up, waiting for the attack. As far as they could see,
there were only the two. It looked like an older man with a
young woman. The bully in James came to the fore as he esti-
mated the odds. They were walking slowly, as if they had very
little strength. "A ruse," he thought sarcastically. Both trappers
motioned the two Beothuk to keep back, but they kept coming.
"More fool them, then ... They asked for it!"

Within seconds, the two Beothuk lay dead in the snow.

Chapter 1
Strange Ships Arrive in the Land of the Beothuk

he Beothuk met solemnly in council to discuss the strange sightings off the coast. Was this what had been prophesied? They discussed the stories handed down to them over the centuries. Their oral history told of tall white-skinned bearded people who had appeared in the northwest many years ago and then left suddenly. They had come over the horizon of the great sea, where no land was known to exist. They skimmed the water like birds swooping on the wing. The wise ones of those days of old had warned that others like them would come in the future. "When that happens, test out the spirits," they had said. "Some of the newcomers will be sent by evil ones, beware of those who try to take possession of the land."

The present apparitions were similar to the descriptions of those in the past, but they were much larger. They, too, floated on water like birds, but were monstrous. Their many wings snatched the wind and forced it to their bidding. When the wind struggled to escape, they snapped and scolded and held it fast. The noise was like tremendous slaps with a huge invisible stick that could be heard for miles. They travelled with frightening speed, and without fear, through the raging seas. Those who had seen them had felt weak with foreboding.

Were they from this world? Or were they beings from beyond the skies, that had landed far out in the ocean and glided towards these shores? Why had they come? The tribe sat around the ceremonial fire, robed in full regalia of feathers and red ochre, and chanted for spiritual guidance. They fasted, prayed for wisdom, and shared their visions. These beings were powerful spirits indeed, spirits who had to be placated. But, at the same time, the Beothuk had to take control of the extraordinary energy released by them.

As one old man spoke, the five six-foot tall shamanic emblems — symbols of the most sacred of beliefs — cast long shadows across the gathering. They knew then what must be done. With solemn respect, another carving was made in the shape of a great ship with two masts, and was set on an identical six-foot stave, along with the other five symbolic images. The carving was then anointed with red ochre and placed with the others before the chief's *mammateek* (the Beothuk word for wigwam).

No one could guess that with the appearance of European sailing vessels on the horizon, the lives of the Beothuk would be profoundly altered, forever. Within 500 years, their coming would result in a path of destruction and in terrifying change for the inhabitants of the island until — at the end — not one would be left.

The first Europeans to come were adventurers and explorers. They were excited about the discovery of the New World, and curious about every aspect of it. Royalty and the powerful merchants the explorers represented waited impatiently for news. Were there magnificent treasures and boundless natural resources to be claimed and plundered? What minerals, timber, flora, and fauna would the new lands yield? Would they be comparable to European species? Would there be enough to replenish the depleting European resources that had been drained at an alarming rate by rapidly expanding populations? Were there magnificent treasures, towns, and castles? What troops would be needed to take them?

When no cities, castles, or empires were evident along the Atlantic seaboard of North America, it came as a huge and encouraging surprise. These unknown lands were obviously ripe for the picking. They had never been mapped and measured, nor had they been developed or improved by a civilized people. It was the duty of Christian men to undertake these tasks for king, for country, and for God.

It soon became apparent that no human beings lived in the New World either. Certainly there were human-like creatures, but they were thought to be so "savage" and their social organization so "primitive" that they were considered less than human. These "savages" knew nothing of oxen, horses, draft animals, ploughs, or wheels. They did not live in houses, but quickly threw up shelters as they moved from place to place. They did no useful work, but indulged themselves all day in the sport of hunting and fishing, just as if they were the idle aristocracy. These creatures were squatters, not worthy of the land they occupied.

The tribulations for the Native peoples began as early as 1498, with a series of abductions, when John Cabot carried some individuals off to England. He presented them to Henry VII and his court. Three years later another group was taken to England, this time by some Bristol merchants. And about the same time John Cabot's son, Sebastian, arrived back home with "sundry people." Friends and relatives of these Native people had no idea where their loved ones would be taken, apart from the fact that they had been forced aboard an alien ship manned by fierce strangely-dressed men, who spoke a garbled tongue and carried devastating weapons. They did know that their kinsmen would never be seen again.

Their European captors gave very little thought to the distress of their victims. They were mere curiosities. Dressed in skins, feathers in their hair, swarthy and foreign looking, the "Red Indians" titillated the imagination of whoever saw them. When displayed at court they could be counted on to amuse the courtiers, and when they were paraded in the marketplace the rabble would pay a few pence for the sight of them. Later, they could be used as slaves. A profitable enterprise, whichever way one looked at it.

The pace of abductions stepped up. In 1501, the Portuguese explorer Corte Reale captured 50 men and women and carried them off to Portugal and slavery. Similarly, the Spaniard Estavao Gomes took 58 captives back with him. In 1507, a French fishing crew grabbed seven people from a birchbark canoe off the east coast of Newfoundland. Only one survived, a boy, who was paraded before the court of Louis XI, the king of France.

Whether or not all these captives were Beothuk is not so important as the fact that these activities were widespread enough to cause deep alarm among the Native peoples. By the early 1500s, fishing crews and other newcomers entering the coastal waters of Newfoundland or Labrador noticed increasingly hostile attitudes. In 1529, Crignon, a French sea captain from Dieppe, reported that "a cruel and austere people with whom it was impossible to converse" populated the south coast of Newfoundland. It was impossible to converse largely because the Beothuk had learned that it was wiser to flee at the sight of a European. Unfortunately, the more elusive they were, the more enticing it became to catch sight of or, even better, to capture one of the inhabitants of this "New-Founde-Land." The Beothuk became the target of popular interest from abroad. And in 1536, an Englishman, Hoare, organized a trip for a party of gentlemen who wanted to discover the "strange things" of the world.

The Atlantic crossing took more than two months. When they spotted "savages" on the shore (probably at Bonavista Bay), everyone on board wanted to see the "natural" people of the country. The crew launched a boat to capture some. The "savages" became alarmed and fled. The crew went ashore anyway, and rifled the camp. They found part of a bear roasting on a wooden spit, a decorated leather boot, and a winter mitten. When the Native people did not return, the disappointed gentlemen sailed off.

By the 1530s the New World's early explorers were recounting stories of waters teeming with fish, of forests abundant with fur-bearing animals, and much more. This created a great stir of interest in Europe. Merchants from competing nations rushed to take advantage of the dazzling opportunities. Fishermen from England, France, Portugal, and Spain set out to find out for themselves. To their astonishment they found such vast stocks of cod off the Newfoundland coast that the waters were alive with leaping fish. The market was so lucrative that fishing vessels began to make annual voyages across the Atlantic to the Grand Banks. Soon there were fleets of ships, all fiercely competing with each other. The catches were sold in Europe where there was a great demand for dried fish. Once cod was cured it could be preserved for years, the perfect food for armies on the march. The fishing crews took over entire stretches of coast where the Beothuk had gathered food for centuries. They gave little thought to the people they displaced, other than to worry whether or not they might be dangerous.

The numbers of these intruders appalled the Beothuk. By the 1550s, up to 50 fishing boats could be seen plying the coast between May and October each year. Between them they carried approximately 1250 people. Their numbers were significant compared with the local Native people who, it is estimated, numbered only 1000 to 2000 at the most.

By 1594, the fleets more than doubled in size. Roughly 100 English ships were fishing along the Newfoundland coast, and the fleets of other European nations were, at times, even larger. It was bad enough that the fishing vessels controlled the fish stocks offshore. What caused the most friction with the Beothuk was that more and more fishermen came ashore. This prevented the Beothuk from accessing the plentiful seafood along the coast, seafood that was necessary for their survival.

The sojourns ashore came about because the English fishermen did not have access to large stocks of salt. The Portuguese and French did, and were able to process fish on board by heavily salting the flesh. The English were forced to cure their catches by a different method. This involved going ashore, splitting and lightly salting the fish, then drying them in the open air on flakes (wooden racks) until they were dehydrated enough to preserve them. These flakes on shore were semi-permanent structures. Large numbers of nearby trees were cut down in order to build them.

The Beothuk did not know what to do. All their experience with European ships told them not to go near the outsiders. When they realized that the fleets customarily sailed away around October each year, they began to retreat into the interior until the fall. Then they would move back to the shore until the ships arrived again in the spring. This definitely had an adverse effect on their seasonal pattern of gathering food, but they decided that it was not worth risking a confrontation. Each time the Beothuk returned they were excited to find rich pickings in the deserted tilts and stages. When the Europeans departed they sometimes dropped knives or left scissors and metal pots behind. Metals were a valuable discovery for the Natives, and they soon learned how to work them. By burning down the structures the Europeans had erected, the Beothuk were able to collect enough nails to fashion a variety of points, arrowheads, and tools.

When the fishermen returned each May and found the ruins, they were furious. It was expensive to ship replacement materials from Europe. In addition, reconstruction wasted time that could have been spent on fishing, and the season was short. They had left their possessions over the winter in the belief that they would be untouched. Weathered, perhaps, but not stolen or destroyed. This seemed to the fishermen to be another instance of the "savages" having no idea of moral values or proper behaviour. In Europe, stealing even minor items (such as a loaf of bread) was a serious crime that carried severe consequences. A thief might be punished by having a hand amputated, by being exported to a penal colony, or even by hanging. Stealing was no small matter.

What to the Beothuk was a windfall — wasted resources that should be scavenged — was to the Europeans an act of war. The fishermen were filled with fierce indignation and a desire for revenge. However, the Beothuk worldview was entirely different from theirs. Tribal cultures around the world have usually had a pragmatic attitude towards possessions. Their lifestyle, dependent on respect for the natural environment, required a frugal attitude. What could be used should be used, and not allowed to waste.

The pilfering by the Beothuk may have inadvertently helped to trigger settlement in Newfoundland, something the Europeans had initially decided not to undertake. Frustrated merchants began to station guards year round to fend off the Red Indians over the winter months. However, these fishing fleets often caused much more havoc for each other than the Beothuk caused. The various competing crews stole each other's boats, removed the ownership marks, and cut them up for wood. They also burned or destroyed their competitors' fishing stages, removed bait from nets or from boats at night, and set fire to the woods.

It is possible that a better understanding might have developed between the Beothuk and the fishermen if the Beothuk had been willing to trade in furs. In other areas, fishing vessels often seized the opportunity for additional income by trading goods for furs with the Native population. Whatever the reason, as early as the end of the sixteenth century the Beothuk generally ignored the chance to do this. Settlement on a small scale became increasingly desirable for the Europeans, although there was still a strong resistance by investors to allow a colony. The Basques created sealing and whaling stations along the northern coast, and monopolized this area. The French built a small fishing colony at Plaisance on the south shore, with fortifications, a garrison, a governor, and several hundred people. The English developed small outports to protect their fishing interests on the southeast coast.

The Beothuk were increasingly dismayed by the invasion of their territory. The best chance for maintaining their lifestyle and living in peace seemed to be withdrawal. Newfoundland was a large island and the interior, with its swampy barrens and dense forests, was difficult to reach for people not used to the terrain. In time the Beothuk pulled out of the Avalon Peninsula so completely that the English came to believe that they had never lived there. This was such a predominant belief that, as late as the fall of 1994, archaeologists were astonished to find Beothuk artifacts under the ruins of one of the major English colonies, at Ferryland.

When the first ships were sighted, 200 years earlier, the Beothuk had been afraid that the ancient prophecies might be upon them. Why were the Beothuk so afraid? To protect the tribe from the consequences of mixing with evil invaders, generation after generation had been indoctrinated from birth. They were taught that any Beothuk who fraternized with wicked spirits (now understood to be white people and Mi'kmaq) must be burned to death at the stake. This ritual of collective purification was so solemnly revered that the punishment continued even beyond death. Once cast out from the tribe, the spirit of the condemned one was forever denied access to the Beothuk lands of the dead. Captive Beothuk agonized over the dilemma this presented. If they had been taken prisoner (through no fault of their own), would they still be outcast? What if the English tried to return them to their tribe?

As time went on, settlers who would have liked to establish friendly relationships with the Beothuk found their attempts almost inexplicably blocked. They were never able to understand why, and as the tribe's numbers dwindled, frantic attempts were made to contact them.

Chapter 2
Blight Descends on the Land

The history of contact between settlers and Beothuk in Newfoundland is rife with misunderstanding brought about by ignorance of each other's culture and worldview. One of the first momentous contacts, the tragic event that followed John Guy's attempt to trade in furs, strongly influenced the Beothuk in their choice to isolate themselves from further contact.

In 1610, permission was finally granted to settle a permanent colony at Cupids, on Conception Bay. The fact that no "savages" had been seen in the area for a long time was a deciding factor in choosing that location. Even so, the settlers were warned in advance not to interfere with the Beothuk if they should encounter them, and not to let the Beothuk inside their homes if they tried to visit the colony.

The authorities believed that a glimpse of European luxury would surely fill the Red Indians with envy, and inspire them to plunder the settlement.

When John Guy first arrived at Cupids with 39 fellow colonists they intended to be self-sufficient, but soon found their expenses much higher than anticipated. The solution seemed to lie in initiating a profitable fur trade with the elusive Native people. John Guy, their leader, sent out two reconnaissance parties on foot to explore an area of Trinity Bay where some mammateeks had been spotted. The overland route proved so difficult that neither group reached their destination. The men returned haggard, exhausted, and discouraged. They had never experienced anything like this in Europe.

Guy then decided to try travelling by sea. His departure was delayed by pirate activity in the area, but he eventually set off on October 7, 1612. With 18 men from the settlement, Guy headed for the same destination the earlier parties had attempted. They took two boats, a barque (a ship with four masts) and a smaller shallop (a boat used in shallow water). From time to time they went ashore to explore the lay of the land. When they came across Native dwellings that looked as if they were still inhabited, they left a few goods inside and took away small items of food or clothing, to signify that they wished to trade. This sea route, too, proved hazardous, as there were dangerous shoals all along the coast. Several times fierce winds forced the shallop to tow the barque, using the power of the shallop's oars to aid the heavier vessel. As they cautiously proceeded, they came across a number of seemingly deserted Beothuk camps. These they freely explored, and at one location they stole a new canoe, which they planned to send back to England as a trophy. It did not occur to them that the Beothuk might view this behaviour as provocative.

When at last they suspected that there were Beothuk nearby watching them, they hoisted a white flag to attract their attention, and to show that they were on a peaceful mission. In response, eight Native people, who until now had remained hidden, lit a signal fire, then paddled closer in two canoes. When the Beothuk gestured for the colonists to come ashore with them, the two larger boats advanced towards the canoes. This made the Beothuk nervous, and they began to leave. Guy again waved the white flag vigorously and dropped the barque's anchor. The Beothuk paused. At this point the captain of the barque was rowed ashore in the shallop. After a while five colonists, led by John Guy, joined the captain. The small group stood together, waiting.

The Beothuk were separated from the party of colonists by a river. After some hesitation, a number of them waded over, leaving guards with the two canoes. John Guy later described the scene in his journal. He wrote that they looked magnificent, their plaited black hair entwined with feathers, with one tall feather standing erect above the crown of their heads. They stood bold and upright, dressed in short leather gowns (the fur turned inwards) with detachable sleeves and beaver skin collars. All were lavishly daubed with red ochre. As they advanced, one of the warriors saluted, pulled off his mittens, and kissed the tip of his fingers towards them. So began an enchanted encounter. At first, when the two groups cautiously mingled, the Beothuk addressed the colonists with long speeches, aided by dramatic gestures, which the English could only guess the meaning of. They seemed friendly. One of the Beothuk shook a white wolf skin during the proceedings. The colonists remained politely attentive until the speeches ended.

Then, suddenly, everyone was dancing. Native people and whites circled together holding hands, leaping, and singing. The Beothuk also beat enthusiastically on their chests and on those of their new partners. Exhausted at last, they settled down to share a meal. The colonists brought out food from the barque, chiefly bread, butter, raisins, aquavitae (similar to brandy), and beer. The Beothuk produced dried caribou meat and a root. As the party grew merry, one of the Beothuk blew into the aquavitae bottle. When it made a snorting sound, everyone fell into laughter.

As the night wore on, they exchanged the flag for the wolf skin, and presented each other with numerous goods. The Beothuk gave presents and furs, and received (perhaps with surprise) a linen cap, 2 hand towels, 3 knives, a small piece of brass, a shirt, 2 table napkins, gloves, 12 spikes, a hatchet, a knife, 4 threaded needles, and a pair of scissors.

Finally, the Beothuk made it clear that the settlers would be safe when they retired for the night. Before they parted, they agreed to meet again in one year's time, at the same spot.

Sadly, this agreement led to a most unfortunate event a year later. In 1613, Guy sent out 10 men to renew contact with the Beothuk at Trinity Bay. As well as initiating trade, he also wanted to get information from them on their way of life. He was especially intent on finding out how the Beothuk dealt with scurvy because it was a major cause of death and disablement among settlers. The trading party left in January, encountering such deep snow that they lost heart and returned home after two days. At this point John Guy sailed to England, intending to return before long. However, he must have found better opportunities in Bristol (he later became its mayor), because Guy left the settlement for good in March that same year.

Apparently the Beothuk did honour their mutual agreement, and waited on shore for the expected ship. A passing fishing boat, ignorant of the arrangement, heard the shouts from the shore and thought the group was hostile. They fired into the crowd. The Beothuk, who viewed this as an act of vile treachery, never forgot this incident. They began to commit acts of revenge whenever the opportunity arose. They also firmly turned their backs on trading furs with the Europeans.

As sad as this misunderstanding was, it is not surprising that the sailors were trigger-happy. These were dangerous times for all. Armed fishing crews and squadrons of warships not only had to keep a sharp eye on each other and on myriad foreign and domestic enemies, but they also shared the waters with reckless pirates who preyed on shipping and coastal settlements. The Beothuk began to dread the constant boom of cannon and the whistle of shot, both from the sea and on land.

The pirates plied the North American eastern seaboard. They sometimes took up the rogues' life almost by chance. Captain Peter Easton, who became a particularly notorious buccaneer, started out loyal to the English Crown. He had been commissioned by Queen Elizabeth I to enforce peace among the lawless fishermen along the Newfoundland coast. When the queen's successor, James I, reduced the size of England's navy, Easton and others were stranded in Newfoundland without pay. Outraged, most of the English officers took an oath of blood brotherhood and seized control of the British warships under their command. From a fort on a small island at Harbour Grace Bay, Captain Easton raided settlements and looted merchant shipping along the Newfoundland coast. He was dreaded for the cruelty with which he frequently press-ganged other sailors into his private navy.

With the coming of the ships, blight seemed to settle over the land. The foul odours carried by the wind were symbolic of the rot that pervaded the frenzy of activity on the beaches. No Beothuk, whether man, woman, or child, could safely go to the small coves that indented the southern Avalon Peninsula. Wherever they were seen, they were shot at. But they were there — always observing, acutely attuned to danger, often hungry — awaiting their chance to scrounge for food.

It was frustrating for the Beothuk to see the constant traffic of small boats rowing out to the great ships, then carrying load after load of fish back to shore. There was arrogance in the boldness with which the fishermen plunged through the churning surf. So intense was the activity between the ships offshore and the hastily erected structures clustered at the beach, that they almost seemed connected by an invisible cord. Strangely dressed men jostled and swore, and wielded sharp knives and shovels as they split and salted the fish. They spread endless amounts of fish onto their racks, from earliest light to dusk. And every morning they began again, spreading and turning the catch on the flakes to dry, forever rowing back to the ships for more. Meanwhile, the Beothuk faced an ever-increasing shortage of food.

Perhaps the most frightening change the Beothuk experienced was the radical alteration of the landscape around the newly settled colonies, such as Ferryland. In 1621, George Calvert purchased a large parcel of land on the coast, about 80 kilometres south of St. John's. The erection of buildings at Ferryland so altered the landscape that it must have seemed to the Native peoples that Mother Earth had become possessed. In contrast with the simple and mobile way of life practiced by the Beothuk, who constructed new homes in an hour or two, from materials at hand, the Europeans settled permanently in one spot. Within a year's time the Beothuk were stunned as they witnessed a frenzy of construction on buildings that challenged their reality. First, there appeared a large mansion with staircases leading to an upper storey. It had an enormous fireplace with a chimney, and a thatched roof that was constructed with rushes from the harbour. Soon there was a brew house, a tavern, saltworks, a forge, and a deep stone well. By 1625 there were 100 permanent residents, including the first women and children. Among them were workmen, such as stonelayers, slaters, carpenters, a saltmaker, and a blacksmith, who engaged in activities never before witnessed by the Beothuk. Even worse, the settlement was visited seasonally by a large number of fishing vessels and their rowdy crews.

What was most shocking was the careless devastation of the land itself. In a short time almost the entire area had become deforested after over 500 trees were cut down. Almost as soon as the colonists landed, there was a bustle of activity and the rasping of saws. Not only were building supplies needed, but also there was an urgent demand for firewood. This harsh climate was much more severe than the settlers had experienced before.

From the earliest settlement, the dwelling complex extended to a harbour with wharves and a large stone sea wall. The location was ideal for easy access to the inshore fishing grounds, and had cobble beaches suitable for drying fish. However, its assets made it vulnerable and the entire area was heavily fortified because of the perceived need for defence.

A menacing palisade of sharpened stakes, 2.13 metres high, completely surrounded four acres. This huge enclosure contained not only buildings, but also fields sown with crops such as barley, oats, peas, and beans that had never been grown there before. A smaller kitchen and salad garden was laid out with foreign fruits and plants. The Beothuk, however, were even more suspicious of the animals. Byres (sheds) and hen houses sheltered cows, pigs, and colourful noisy birds. These imported species were not natural to the environment. Land had to be devoted to feeding them, so a three-acre meadow was given over to hay. The defences were soon justified. The settlement became a focus of political interest from far beyond the locality. In 1675 the Dutch, angry at losing their colonies at New Amsterdam (now New York), retaliated against the English by raiding the coast of North America. They arrived at Ferryland with four ships, set fire to buildings, drove off the livestock, burned 30 boats in the harbour, and took as much fish as their ships could carry. The inhabitants were forced to provide six hogs and one bullock to each ship in return for the Dutch sparing the rest of the settlement.

Twenty years later the French, from the colony at Plaisance, launched an even more merciless raid. They not only attacked from the sea, but also sent troops overland through Beothuk territory. The devastation was so complete that the colony was depopulated and the inhabitants forced back to England. After a year some came back, and the struggle for survival began all over again as the settlement was slowly rebuilt.

It isn't hard to imagine what the Beothuk felt when they saw the drama taking place before their eyes on such a broad scale. They were powerless to change events. A confrontation would be foolhardy. The invaders were merciless in using deadly weapons, not only guns but also cannons. The Beothuk never did acquire guns, perhaps because, in this too, they did not want to engage in trade with the invaders.

Although the various Beothuk bands and family groups were not organized to act in unity in day-to-day activities, they did come together intentionally each fall at Red Indian Lake. There they collaborated as one people in a massive caribou hunt, participated in spiritual celebrations, and deliberated matters of significance for the entire tribe. The Beothuk knew they must focus, as they had from time immemorial, on finding food enough for all to share. Their most urgent need was to maintain their freedom to hunt and gather in the remote forests and isolated shores in safety.

Newfoundland probably seemed vast enough to the Beothuk to allow them to lead separate lives from the fishing communities and the colonists. The escalation of hostile events must have made retreat seem an attractive option.

In the autumn, in the most secret recesses of the forest, deep inland beside the greatest of the lakes and waterways, they crowded around the fires of the main camp. In the presence of the sacred staves and the carved emblem of a

European ship, they celebrated their faith and renewed their principles and beliefs. And it was there, during these ceremonial gatherings, that the various bands, as one, trained their children to be ever wary of the long-anticipated enemy.

Chapter 3
Hemmed in From Every Side

T he Beothuk's gradual withdrawal from the Avalon Peninsula, the area most subject to the overland forays of armed troops and the presence of hostile fleets, was a tribal decision. However, not long after, other factors outside their control forced them into a deeper retreat. Eventually, almost the entire coastline was affected by foreign activity. The Beothuk pulled back even more — cutting themselves off from the ocean's rich resources — resources on which their lives depended.

Starvation was a constant threat. Their existence was an endless round of attempts to manage and balance the seasonal variations. If, during a one-year cycle, the weather pattern altered dramatically, or some unforeseen event changed caribou migration patterns, it could create a serious food crisis for the Beothuk. In order to gather enough to survive during both winter and summer, it was necessary to travel to where food was most plentiful at any given time. The tribe traditionally spent the spring and summer among the indented bays and the countless islands offshore. They foraged in small family bands concentrating on collecting wild bird eggs, and hunted animals such as hare, marten, fox, bear, and seal. The bands also fished, and they harpooned the seal at sea from open boats, which was often extremely dangerous.

The bulk of their food was dried or preserved so that it could be stocked for winter and easily carried on their travels. In the fall, when most of the bands left the coast to go deep inland to the Exploits complex of rivers and lakes, it was principally to hunt the huge caribou herds that annually migrated through this area. During this event the Beothuk collaborated to build fences to control the places where caribou crossed the rivers. There they could be slaughtered easily at chosen sites without needless waste. These fences extended over many miles, a dense breastplate of cut trees and twigs, towering well over a man's head. They were vital to the gathering of food resources, and their repair and extension depended on an organized community effort.

After the mass kill, hundreds of carcasses were frozen then packaged and stored in pits at the main camp on Red Indian Lake. The meat was shared by all alike. The tribe also fished for salmon, which was bountiful in the Exploits and its tributaries and was an essential source of food for the

Beothuk. Their three major winter camps at Red Indian Lake were extremely difficult for outsiders to access. But for the Beothuk, who had been raised in the difficult terrain, the three camps were within easy trekking distance of each other.

The dwellings at the Red Indian Lake winter camps were very different from the quickly erected mammateeks they used in their summer travels. The winter houses were large, semi-subterranean, multi-sided structures, sometimes up to 10 metres in diameter. They could hold up to 50 or 60 people. Each dwelling was warmly insulated with moss and clay, and had a central fireplace with an opening above for smoke to escape. There were lofts for storage, and personal belongings hung on the walls. There were additional fire pits outside, and hundreds of caribou leg bones were mounted on poles throughout the camp. Deep food storage pits contained frozen meat.

The five ceremonial staves with their shamanic emblems were always planted outside the chief's mammateek. During the great annual feasts and spiritual celebrations, every infant who had been born within the year was anointed with grease and red ochre at an initiation ceremony. At these times, all the adults from every family also renewed their own ochre anointments, which affirmed their tribal identity. The entire nation had sung and danced at these central gatherings, safe from predators for hundreds of years ....

Then, in the 1700s, a number of changes took place almost simultaneously. First, the English began to settle permanently, and move inland to build large commercial salmon fisheries in the heart of Red Indian territory. Trappers also encroached farther and farther inland. Second, during the 1700s the Mi'kmaq began to infiltrate Newfoundland in ever increasing numbers. They had made the ocean crossing by canoe from Cape Breton for hundreds of years, but they were so few initially that they were no threat to the Beothuk. Mutual respect and friendship developed and the two peoples some-times joined together for celebrations. This situation changed radically after the French forged a strong military alliance and trading relationship with the Mi'kmaq on the mainland. This opened the door for the French colony in Newfoundland at Plaisance to play the Mi'kmaq off against their local enemies, the Beothuk and the English. They supplied the Mi'kmaq with firearms, and since the Beothuk refused to adopt guns, the odds became desperately unequal.

There were significant battles between the two tribes. The Beothuk, lacking firepower, suffered major defeats and were forced to retreat inland from the St George's Bay area. Within 30 years there was a violent confrontation at the northern end of Grand Lake. The Mi'kmaq won, and tradi-tion says they put every man, woman, and child to death. Whatever the truth, this victory gave them control over the whole of the western region of Newfoundland. In the south of Newfoundland, the Mi'kmaq, largely because of their close ties with the French at Plaisance, now dominated the hunt-ing and fishing around the harbours west of Placentia Bay.

Although the official English position was that they were "foreign Indians" and must return to "their own side of the gulf" in Nova Scotia by October of each year, only a few obeyed. Instead, they moved determinedly inland, advancing from the south as far as Exploits River, into the heart of Beothuk territory. And the Mi'kmaq began to hunt in the same areas as the ever-encroaching English trappers.

Beothuk numbers began to dwindle with the relentless fighting and atrocities. They fought back with small raids and the random killings of individual Mi'kmaq and settlers. The Beothuk practice of decapitating captives, putting their heads on poles, and dancing around them terrified both the Mi'kmaq and the English. Their horrifying deeds became legendary and fear of the tribe was widespread.

The Beothuk faced another challenge when the Inuit (who were particularly hostile to the Beothuk) and the Montagnais moved into the Northern Peninsula. This occurred around the same time that the French sealing stations in the north began to restrict Beothuk access to that part of the coast. The result was that the Beothuk were caught in a multilateral squeeze that forced them farther into the interior. They were cut off from the vital resources of the coast that ensured a varied diet.

The English posed the most devastating of all these threats. They steadily advanced inland into Beothuk territory, taking over the salmon rivers and disturbing the caribou migration patterns through their random hunting. And they quickly became major competitors for all fur-bearing animals. At first, when the settlers took only what they needed for their own consumption, the Beothuk still had enough fish to meet their needs. Then, in 1708, an entrepreneur named George Skeffington constructed a very large commercial salmon fishery to cure and process salmon for export and took control over several of the major salmon rivers in the interior. The Beothuk depended on these for fish, especially the Gander, the Exploits, and the Indian Arm Rivers.

Skeffington not only built houses and fishing stages, but various settlers had miles of forest cleared along the banks in order to service and patrol the salmon posts. A mix of bullying and the threat of firearms scared off the Beothuk. Even worse, the English, greedy to harvest the fish in record time, dammed rivers and set up weirs to prevent salmon from reaching the spawning grounds. The fish were forced to congregate in the pools below, where waiting salmon catchers scooped them out in huge numbers. Fleets of nets were set along the Exploits for at least 44 kilometres.

For the first time, the Beothuk retaliated with organized violence. Around 1720, they broke down weirs, took away nets and provisions, and killed some of Skeffington's men. In response, Skeffington raised a posse of 30 to 40 armed men, and the Beothuk retreated except for occasional lightning raids.

The operation of the fishery was then greatly extended into most areas of Notre Dame Bay. The Beothuk were left with access to only a few small rivers, including Charles Brook. Soon the salmon catchers had moved in there, too. In response, the Beothuk patrolled the river in several large canoes. The settlers were alarmed, knowing that they were being watched from the surrounding forest. Sometimes Beothuk appeared on the opposite bank, making threatening gestures and shouting. None of these settlers were harmed though, and the Beothuk again pulled back from Notre Dame Bay, this time almost entirely. Edward Burd noted in his journal in 1726, "The Indians are now pretty much worn out ... the English ... treat them with great severity."

Now seriously threatened by the scarcity of a staple in their diet, the Beothuk reacted much more forcefully. They mounted determined raids, especially at night (which particularly frightened the settlers) and initiated a kind of guerrilla warfare of ambush and random killing. The settlers reacted by sending out equally random punitive raiding parties. Colonists were particularly vulnerable to attack while at work, likely because it served as a message to desist from these destructive activities. Two young men were ambushed on their way to take salmon out of a pond at Ragged Harbour. One was killed, and the other one escaped when he managed to reach his gun and wound one of the attackers.

Thomas Rowsell, who had the reputation of being a great "Indian killer" who never spared the lives of any Native people, was killed while he was dipping salmon at his weir in New Bay. His body was found stripped naked, pierced with arrows, and beheaded. In retaliation, eight of Rowsell's friends ambushed a party of Beothuk in two canoes at Moore's Cove and riddled them with buckshot. Several were killed.

In the early 1760s, shipmaster Scott and his fishing crew built a fortified house in the Bay of Exploits. One day the premises were surrounded by a large number of Beothuk, and Scott went out unarmed to investigate. Trying to put on a show of friendliness, he attempted to mix with them even though they were clearly a well-armed raiding party. An old Native man, pretending to respond in a friendly way, put his arms around Scott's neck. As he did so, another warrior stabbed Scott in the back. The Beothuk launched into bloodcurdling war whoops, and let loose a storm of arrows. The other shipmaster and four crewmembers were killed before the rest escaped to the ships. On another occasion, five Englishmen who tried to settle in Hall's Bay were attacked by a war party. This time their heads were cut off and stuck on poles.

As well as being known for their chilling ferocity in beheading captives, the Beothuk also had a reputation for being unexpectedly merciful. On one occasion, a fisherman in the Bay of Exploits was inspecting his traps along a riverbank when he heard a voice. Startled, he looked up and saw a Beothuk standing on the shore with an arrow notched into his bow, ready to shoot. He signalled to the fisherman to leave, and the man rowed away as fast as if the devil was after him. Boasting about his adventure later, he claimed to regret not having had his gun with him, as he would have shot the Beothuk "dead upon the spot." This was quite consistent with the prevailing attitude of the settlers.

Furriers, in contrast with fishermen, tended to trap alone. If they could, trappers might open fire on Native people, but just as often they snuck away if they came upon a group. On the other hand, there is not one report of a Beothuk killing a trapper on his trapline or in his tilt, although there was plenty of opportunity. They did, however, enjoy sleuthing trappers and scaring them by hiding around their tilts, and they did take their traps. When one trapper, Richard Richmond, found fresh tracks around his tilt and all his traps missing, he was frightened enough to leave permanently.

William Cull did not give up so easily. He saw tracks near his tilt at Peters Brook, but he only had his hatchet with him, so he rushed back to get his gun. He then loaded it with drop shot, hurriedly put on his snowshoes, and set off in pursuit, ready to kill. Cull tracked the offenders for two full days before giving up the chase. Not willing to give them the slightest satisfaction, he collected whatever traps he could carry, and then destroyed all the rest before he returned home.

The Beothuk were never given credit for their considerable restraint. But some of the settlers, outraged at their losses, planned elaborate revenge. They made indiscriminate raids on Beothuk camps, stole furs (in one raid over 100 skins were looted), destroyed essentials like mammateeks and canoes, and killed or injured for the sport of it.

John Peyton Sr. and his partner Harry Miller, together with their headman Thomas Taylor, deliberately planned one particularly disturbing raid. In 1781, after walking along the bank of the Exploits for three days, they spied some Beothuk processing caribou skins beside a small camp. The trappers burst in and immediately fired without warning. Men, women, and children, in utter confusion, fled screaming with terror into the shelter of the nearby trees. The men pursued them ruthlessly, and caught a number of the wounded, as well as a young girl and an older woman. There is no record of what they did with those they caught (settlers who were later questioned were very evasive), but it was known that Peyton had 36 pistol balls in his gun. He personally bragged about it as "a glorious expedition," and related that he had discovered an old man in a mammateek who had in his hand one of Peyton's traps, which had been stolen on a previous occasion. He was working it against a rock, fashioning arrowheads from the iron. Peyton wrested what remained of the trap from him and savagely beat his brains out. The trappers then pilfered the camp, and loaded up as many furs as they could carry. They left without any concern for the distress and injury they left behind them.

Nine years later, in 1790, the same Harry Miller sent out eight men on a raid of winter settlements, ostensibly to retrieve stolen traps and salmon nets. The real purpose was additional revenge for Thomas Rowsell's death and beheading. The men travelled for four days until they came across four mammateeks and three canoes in a small cove. The Beothuk, who saw them coming, snatched up the small children and fled into the forest. The men set their dogs on them, and routed out two women and an infant. At first they intended to force the women to go back with them, but later reconsidered and let them go, thinking they would be a burden and not worth the trouble. Meanwhile, they had a hearty meal, bundled up as many skins and possessions as they could carry away, and spent the night in the camp. Before they left in the morning they set fire to three of the four mammateeks and burned all the canoes. In addition, they destroyed or threw into the river any useful articles, as well as those that had previously been stolen from settlers.

Women who were caught alone were often brutalized. One of the most gruesome murders was of a pregnant woman who was shot when she begged on her knees for mercy. Her hands were chopped off and later displayed as a hunting trophy. Another Beothuk woman pleaded for mercy for herself and her two children, exposing her breasts to her captors, John Moore and his friend. (This may have been her way of letting him know that she was a mother or that she was a female.) They killed her and attempted to make off with her children. One child died while it was being hauled to the boat, and the other escaped into the woods.

Settlers constantly challenged the Beothuk, even at sea. Initially, both the Beothuk and the settlers hunted seal from open boats. However, when the English started to use decked schooners for sealing and built large settlements at the mouths of bays, they gained every advantage, eventually destroying the Beothuk's capacity to hunt seal in those areas.

Settlers also harassed the Beothuk when they paddled to the many islands around the coast to collect eggs from the colonies of seabirds that nested there. They went as far afield as Funk Island, which was a considerable distance offshore. When armed colonists also began to collect eggs on a large scale, they enjoyed the sport of holing Beothuk canoes they encountered at sea with mole shot. To avoid their tormentors, the Beothuk waited to put to sea until the water was shrouded by thick fog, a dangerous practice. Not content just to collect the eggs, the English began to decimate the bird population. Feathers were sought after for European clothing and they produced a good price. The Funk Island great auk, in particular, was slaughtered both for its feathers and its thick layer of fat, which was rendered for fuel. These birds could not fly, and they were driven into corrals where they could be easily killed, scalded, and plucked. So many were destroyed that by 1800 the species became extinct.

Viewed from a wider perspective, nearly all the stresses suffered by the Beothuk on their small remote island were inseparable from the shifting European economic and political climate. European power struggles were played out in colonial policies that seldom considered the New World as anything more than an extension of their own interests at home.

After the mid-1700s, another alarming kind of harassment began to take root, the kidnapping of Beothuk children. The ultimate purpose (although this never actually happened) was to place them back with their tribe once they began to conform to the settlers' way of thinking. It was hoped that the tribe might be introduced to Christianity by these means. There was also the chance that once the Beothuk were tamed, the entire island could then be surveyed for its natural resources without undue danger and interference.

At least three children were deliberately abducted and brought up in English households during the 1700s. In 1758, a group of Irish hunters from Fogo opened fire upon a lone mammateek. They killed a woman and child, but a young boy of about nine survived. The English named him Tom June (after the month he was taken). He was initially taken to England, and then later raised in Newfoundland. Subsequently, Tom June was employed in the fishery at Fogo where he became a well-known businessman.

The second child, John August, was kidnapped 10 years after the snatching of Tom June. Some fishermen chanced upon a woman with a child on her back. They shot and killed the woman, but carried off the boy, who was believed to be about four years old. He was presented to Governor Palliser for "a gratuity" (which was probably never paid). The boy was too young to be questioned about his culture, and of course did not understand a word of English. The next year he was taken to England and displayed in a public market for the price of roughly two pence per viewer. John August, also, was later returned to Newfoundland, where he eventually held the responsible position of master of a boat under the employ of a Trinity merchant.

The third and last child intentionally kidnapped was a girl, Oubee, who was taken in July 1791. Three Englishmen came upon what they were sure must have been a case of murder, after they noticed an empty punt (a shallow flat-bottomed boat with square ends) near a mammateek at Charles Brook. In fact, a family of Beothuk had taken the punt after two fishermen stole their canoe. They were forced to walk at least 100 kilometres through the forest to Indian Arm, where they stole the empty punt so that they could get back to their people. The family consisted of two women, two boys, and a young girl. The Englishmen allowed the women to escape, killed the man (who was holding a boy in his arms,) wounded the other boy, and carried off the girl, whose age was estimated as less than 10 years old.

Oubee was raised among the family of Thomas Stone of Trinity. Although they were said to have treated her with considerable care and humanity, she still tried to escape. They caught her anyway. The young girl was old enough to help compile a vocabulary of about 100 important Beothuk words. She did this by giving the name of objects as they were pointed out. These words were the first of the Beothuk language ever recorded. Dr. Clinch, who worked with her on the project, confirmed that "Oubee" was her Beothuk name.

Around 1795, the Stones made a permanent move back to England, taking her with them. Oubee died a very short time after they arrived in England.

The same year that John August was kidnapped, Governor Palliser commissioned Lieutenant John Cartwright to lead an expedition into the interior to try to contact the Beothuk and to render them "useful subjects to his Majesty." Cartwright was genuinely concerned about the plight of the Beothuk, and set off up the Exploits River on August 24, 1768. The heavily armed party went as far as Start Rattle, where they left the boats in the woods and divided into two groups in order to search both banks simultaneously. At the end of four days the conditions were unbearable. Many of the men had worn through their shoes, they had eaten almost all their supplies, and the rain was constant. The majority turned back for the shallop. Five of the original 14 persisted through the rain until sunset, when they erected a shelter for the night. The next morning found them at the edge of Red Indian Lake, where they discovered a large settlement that was almost covered by tall weeds and young trees. It had obviously been deserted for some time. On the way back they passed another more recently occupied camp, but still did not encounter any Beothuk. Cartwright had to be content with the opportunity to map areas that had never been recorded before by a European. He took extensive notes on the flora, fauna, and mineral resources. And, most importantly, he wrote a detailed description of the cultural artifacts the Beothuk had left behind. In this respect, Cartwright's mission was far from a failure, although it had fallen short of its prime objective, which was to befriend the Native peoples. When he failed to encounter even one Beothuk, he began to suspect that they travelled to different areas with the seasons (a fact that was not yet known).

In any case, there was considerable alarm raised when it was reported that the group had found the major camps of the Beothuk deserted. Subsequently, a year later (in 1760), Governor Byron published a proclamation that condemned the persecution of the Beothuk. The proclamation made killing or wounding a Native person punishable by hanging.

Sadly, the proclamation was totally ineffective because the settlers most involved and affected by it did not support it. The atrocities continued.

Chapter 4
The Beheading at Red Indian Lake

Lieutenant John Cartwright put in a compelling report in 1769 stating that, although he had penetrated to their major camps along the Exploits, he had not seen any Beothuk. He wrote that it looked as if the area he explored had been deserted for some time and that he feared the entire tribe was on the verge of extinction. Despite its urgent tone, Cartwright's report had very little impact on the settlers. From time to time successive governors issued further proclamations threatening severe penalties for inhumane treatment of the Native peoples, but they were generally ineffective. There were a number of fishermen and furriers who continued to commit atrocities whenever an opportunity occurred.

A new policy was introduced some time later. A reward

of £50 was offered to anyone who captured a Beothuk alive. This strategy was less costly to government than staging a mission and it was designed to motivate the settlers to co-operate. In September 1803, William Cull of Fogo took advantage of this offer and delivered a young Beothuk woman to St John's. He claimed and was given the £50 for his expenses and loss of time. Cull probably assumed that would be the end of it as far as his duties were concerned. He was wrong.

The arrival of the captive Beothuk woman created great excitement in St John's. Cull said that she had been paddling alone in her canoe, headed for a nearby island to collect eggs when he seized her. A great effort was made to make a fuss of her; although neither her own nor an assigned name was ever recorded. She was kindly greeted by Governor Gambier and other dignitaries, and exhibited before a large assembly of principal merchants and their ladies who were invited to meet her at Government House. The Beothuk woman was astonished and acted as though she was pleased by her reception. Although she seemed to enjoy the music played by the band, it was noted that she refused to dance. She was given European clothes to wear, but insisted on keeping her sealskin garments, which were smeared with grease and red ochre, near to her. The people of St John's showered her with gifts, showed her around the shops, and invited her to take whatever she liked. Gold ornaments, feathers, and brightly coloured items particularly caught her fancy.

Onlookers commented on her manners and disposition. She was gentle and kind and responded to affection, and she was fond of children. Over all, she made a very good impression. Considering that she was a captive, she appeared to be relatively content with her situation. It is not known how long this Beothuk woman was kept in St John's. People assumed that, because of the goodwill shown her and her exposure to luxury, she would be convinced that the English way of life was far "superior" to that of her own people.

A plan suddenly materialized to return the Beothuk woman to her people loaded with gifts such as fishing lines, saws, nails, hatchets, knives, kettles, blankets, and shoes. It was assumed she would tell them about the kindly treatment she had received, and that this would go a long way towards "civilizing and improving the condition of [the] miserable creatures." At this point, William Cull was bluntly told to take her back to where he had found her. He was most reluctant to do this and was insulted by the additional £15 awarded him to purchase the goods and to take her back to the wilderness. Cull received his orders without much direction. The release of the Beothuk woman had not been planned and seemed a careless afterthought. The fact that she could not speak English or express her thoughts directly to her captors seemed inconsequential. No one had attempted to elicit information from her as to how many there were in her tribe, where they were located, or how communication might be established. All these questions were thrown instead upon the shoulders of the unwilling William Cull.

When he returned with her to his home in Fogo, he was at a dead end. He had already lost time away from his work, and he knew that the task of returning her was not going to be easy. The journey into the heart of enemy territory was difficult enough, but her gifts must also be transported with her through the wilderness. Further, it was now winter, and he could not find any men willing to go with them. Feeling he had little choice, he decided to keep her at his home in Fogo instead. The government agreed to pay him for her board and lodging. Throughout the long winter months, she taught Cull, his wife, and one of their sons a little of her language. It was just enough for them to be able to explain to her that the English wished to be on friendly terms with her people.

By the spring of 1804, the new governor took matters in hand and arranged for four men to accompany Cull and the woman up the Exploits and deliver her to her people. Meanwhile, Cull had become even more resentful of his task and delayed the journey until August. He and the men assigned to him were greatly afraid of going too close to a Beothuk camp. They compromised by taking her up the river some distance and then leaving her alone in the forest to find the rest of the way back. Ten days later, they checked the place they had left her and found that she had gone. Cull claimed that he believed the Beothuk had rescued her. He then wrote to the governor's secretary to explain what had been done, and to say that he wanted nothing more to do with the Beothuk. Besides the inconvenience he had suffered, he said that he lived among neighbours who often shot Beothuk without hesitation. He had been given the additional duty of bringing offenders guilty of atrocities against the Native peoples back to St John's for trial. He was very uncomfortable with this turn of events, as he was well known for his former animosity towards the Beothuk. He had boasted that he had shot more Indians with his long Fogo duck gun than he could remember.

The Beothuk woman's sudden disappearance raised some unpleasant and awkward questions in St John's. Had her people really taken her off? Or had Cull murdered her? The situation remained controversial until she was later reported to have visited some of the English settlements alone. This in itself was a mystery. Why had she not returned to her own people?

The succeeding governor, Sir John Thomas Duckworth, doubled the reward money to £100. When the Reverend Edmund Violet, a Methodist minister in St John's, suggested sending a formal mission into the interior, to be led by a man of perseverance and humane motive, Governor Duckworth listened attentively. The objective was to foster a peaceful co-existence, develop trading relations, and get valuable information on the resources of the country, which were still substantially unexplored.

In full agreement with this proposal, Governor Duckworth appointed Lieutenant David Buchan, commander of the HMS *Adonis*, to lead the expedition, both because of his character and because he was experienced with winter travel in the interior. The governor gave Buchan a free hand to deal with circumstances as he saw fit. Lieutenant Buchan set off up the Exploits River at 7 a.m. on January 13, 1811, with 23 heavily armed marines, and three local settlement guides, one of whom was (once more) William Cull. They journeyed up the river for 11 days, attempting roughly 12 kilometres a day, and camped each night in makeshift shelters. Paralyzed by cold, they had to battle numbing winds and freezing sleet. Progress was difficult. Sometimes sledges had to be unpacked and dragged up steep banks while the load was carried by hand, and some of the sledges became too damaged to use. In addition to extreme fatigue, swollen and inflammed legs added to the men's misery.

When they finally reached the upper part of the river, they discovered old campsites as well as miles of caribou fences, which lined both banks. On the 11th day, open water forced them to reconsider. Since the sledges could go no farther, Buchan now set off with half the party, carrying only enough supplies for four days.

Buchan's party soon came across fresh tracks that they believed to be Beothuk. These led around a point to a large frozen lake. At nightfall, they paused to take shelter in the woods. It was extraordinarily cold. At 4 a.m., warmed and cheered by a dram of rum, they set out again, trying their utmost to not make a sound. Along the way, they passed large numbers of frozen caribou carcasses. Finally, they crossed the lake and were startled by the sight of six canoes and three mammateeks. Seeing the dwellings, and believing them to be occupied, the marines stealthily climbed the bank and formed into three groups.

When Buchan called out and there was no answer, they removed the skins at one of the dwelling entrances. Howley's book, *The Beothuks or Red Indians* (1915), records Buchan's impression of the scene: "We beheld a group of men, women, and children lying in the utmost consternation; they were some minutes without motion or utterance."

The English party, too, were momentarily speechless. It was up to Buchan now to obtain their trust. The English shook hands all around, showed their friendliness in every possible way, and paid special attention to the children. He later wrote: "Never were finer infants seen." He counted at least 30, all under the age of six. The women responded by embracing him. Some examined the Englishmen's dress with great curiosity. Others kindled a fire and cooked caribou steaks for the entire party. While they were waiting, Buchan gave them knives, handkerchiefs, and other articles. The Beothuk, in turn, offered the Englishmen skins. "Everything promised the greatest cordiality." After three-and-a-half hours had passed, Buchan tried to indicate that he wanted to return to where he had left his baggage and come back with some more goods. Four of the Beothuk mimed that they would accompany him. Corporal James Butler and Private Thomas Bouthland asked if they could stay behind to repair their snowshoes and

Buchan granted permission. In doing so, he wanted to show the Beothuk his confidence in them.

Buchan and the rest of the men headed back towards their base camp. It was not long before two of the Beothuk (one likely the chief) turned back. The party continued on and had almost reached their destination when a third Beothuk ran away. The fourth continued on with the marines, and seemed pleased when he was shown the gifts at the camp. Meanwhile, Buchan was troubled over why the three Beothuk had run off. The next day eight of the men stayed behind at the base camp. The other 19 and the fourth Beothuk set out once more for the Beothuk camp. When they got there, the mammateeks were deserted and everything looked disordered. The one remaining Beothuk, who was still accompanying them, looked surprised and very uneasy. Buchan became increasingly worried about the safety of Butler and Bouthland, the two men he had left at the Beothuk camp. Using mimed actions, he told the one remaining Beothuk that he was free to go, but urged him to return to the others and ensure that his two marines would not be harmed. The man smiled enigmatically and pointed to the west side of the lake. He didn't leave but went instead to one of the mammateeks. It contained the Beothuk chief's staff, which he showed to Buchan. By this time, feeling deeply anxious that something was terribly wrong, Buchan had placed half of the men on strict guard duty for the night.

Early the next morning (January 26), 14 days after they

had left the schooner, the men placed gifts of blankets, shirts, and tin pots in each of the dwellings and also attached some articles to the chief's staff. They intended to return in two day's time. The Beothuk who was still with them was running ahead, when suddenly he came to a stop and veered off at great speed in a different direction. Buchan looked around to determine what had alarmed him. He was appalled and sickened by what he saw. There lay the naked bodies of his two marines on the ice, pierced by arrows. Their heads had been cut off. There was no trace of their heads or of their clothes. Buchan's men were thrown into shock, which quickly progressed to a blood lust for revenge. Buchan, however, was more concerned for the safety of the eight men they had left behind at their base camp and ordered an immediate retreat. The marines stayed constantly on the alert for an ambush from the forest. When the party at last got back to the base camp, Buchan was immensely relieved to find everything in order and the men safe.

He decided that he must return to the ship without delay, as he anticipated that the Beothuk would be expecting revenge and were likely on the war path. Once again, the retreating expedition encountered extremely hazardous weather conditions. When the sledges finally bogged down, the men were forced to load provisions into knapsacks. They fearfully set off across the inhospitable country, weighed down by their additional burden. The party made it safely back to the *Adonis* within four days, arriving exhausted on January 30.

In spite of the terrible outcome of the expedition, Buchan was still hopeful that the mission could be completed. He ordered new sledges and casks to be built and, after the men had rested, they set out for the second time on March 5, again with 29 men. Now more experienced about what to expect, Buchan paid special attention to each man's clothing and emergency equipment. They carried provisions for 22 days travel. After many delays caused by the continuing extreme weather conditions, they came across a storehouse they had passed on their previous journey. The Beothuk had since removed the best quality meat, dug up the ground, and riddled the hut with arrows. Respecting the fact that the Beothuk were in a militant mood, Buchan took a little of what remained of the meat and left some red shirts in the storehouse in exchange. Then the group headed back to the schooner through deep snow, heavy sleet, and freezing hail. After these two trips into the interior, Buchan was so ill from the hardships they had endured that he was forced to rest. Once he recovered his strength, however, nothing could hold him back. Throughout the following two summers he continued to scout the coast, often spotting fresh traces of the Beothuk. However, they became deeply discouraged when they suffered the constant torment of mosquitoes as they lay in futile wait in the woods.

It was not until almost two decades later, with the capture of three Beothuk women, an old mother and her two daughters, that the Beothuk point of view was brought forward. The youngest captive, Shanawdithit, who survived the capture and remained with the English, later revealed an amazing story ....

Shanawdithit had been at the Beothuk camp when the marines were killed. At that time she was only a child, but years later she talked about the tragic killings. Apparently, the number of Beothuk was much lower than the English had estimated, only 72 in total. Nevertheless, they continued to hunt at their principal haunts of Red Indian Lake and the Exploits River. That winter they were camped in three groups at different parts of the lake. The largest camp, the one that Buchan had come upon, was at the eastern end of the lake. The camp's three mammateeks were occupied by a total of 42 people. Shanawdithit's father headed one of the dwellings, and Shanawdithit was in it at the time the marines burst in on the group.

Far from seeing Buchan's party as friendly, the Beothuk believed that they had been taken prisoner by a hostile force. After several hours, during which both sides mimed, the Beothuk thought that an agreement had been reached to exchange hostages. The Beothuk did not believe that Buchan intended to go back for more supplies. They thought that Buchan intended to return with a larger force to carry them off to the dreaded ships. The tribe grew increasingly consumed by suspicion and anxiety after two of the Beothuk who had left with Buchan returned so precipitously. They had treated the marines, who had stayed with them, kindly, until this moment. But now, faced with their perceived need to make an immediate escape, the band was afraid that the hostages would hamper their movements on the trail. They also thought that if they left them behind at the camp, the marines would betray the direction in which the Beothuk had fled. Shanawdithit said that the tribe was very much divided over the issue of whether or not to kill the men. The chief, who had initially accompanied Buchan, wanted to do it immediately, but others were in vigorous opposition to the idea. While they were arguing, one of the Beothuk men tried to take a jacket off one of the marines. When the marine balked, the matter was suddenly and spontaneously decided. They could not risk the marines' lack of co-operation. Four men immediately took the two men out onto the ice and then shot them with arrows from behind.

Shanawdithit's mother then lopped the heads from the bodies. The band hurriedly packed up and crossed the lake, carrying the two heads with them. They left one head at the north side of the lake, stuck on a pole, then travelled along the shore to the next Beothuk camp. They frantically told the people there what had happened. The second camp joined forces with them, and all of them retreated westward, where the last Beothuk hostage who had accompanied Buchan's party joined them the next day. This man was Shanawdithit's uncle. The two bands crossed the lake once more, and sent a message to the third band, which immediately joined them. The entire group trekked to a remote area inland, taking their winter provisions with them, as they intended to stay the winter in hiding. They built six new mammateeks, and then celebrated together. The second head was impaled on a pole, and the Beothuk danced and sang around it for several hours.

When spring came the Beothuk went back to the largest camp at Red Indian Lake to fetch more supplies of meat. During this journey they went back to where they had left the head of the first marine, and danced and sang ceremoniously around it. They then dispersed into small groups and retreated to remote areas of the island.

Buchan's major mistake had been to underestimate their hostile feelings. This was partly due to the European cultural misperception about Native peoples that was prevalent at the time. Natives were believed to be primitive, childlike, and emotionally underdeveloped. One of Buchan's stated goals had been "to bring the natives into civil society" so that they could be educated in a more sophisticated way of life. In treating them like children, insisting on their accepting presents, and trying to force trust on them, Buchan (and others) took little account of the anger and the feelings of revenge that had boiled up through centuries of mistreatment. His own idealistic and perhaps naïve belief in the Beothuk's ability and willingness to trust him was what ultimately set the scene for tragedy.

Chapter 5
Demasduit's Traumatic Capture

Even after Buchan's expedition to the interior ended in such horror, he was still obsessed with completing his mission, and Governor Duckworth gave him full support. Buchan continued his quest, sometimes sighting Beothuk canoes, but they always slipped away. Occasionally, he came across the ashes of campfires that were still warm, but the people who had lit them fled his approach. Contact constantly eluded him.

War with Great Britain and the United States of America broke out in 1812. These were difficult times in Newfoundland, as famine and dire economic conditions created unrest throughout the colonies. As a result, government control over the northern areas of Newfoundland relaxed, and violence and retaliation continued to flare between the colonists and the Native peoples.

In 1816, John Peyton Sr., in company with two other men, discovered a winter mammateek on the Exploits River, near Rushy Pond. When the settlers attacked, 10 to 12 Beothuk escaped and gathered some distance away on the riverbank. One of the women, however, was caught and mercilessly killed by Peyton Sr.

The next year four men sighted nine Beothuk asleep on a small island. They paddled up quietly and shot all of them. One of them boasted about the murder. A settler, who listened to his tale, was curious enough to investigate and, some time later, found a pile of bleached human bones at that spot. Shanawdithit later said that during that same summer some of her relatives were shot and killed when they were canoeing to an island to collect the eggs of wild birds.

During the same period, the Beothuk stepped up their raids on winter houses and fishing stations. They persistently carried off essential tools, which were hard to replace, especially in wilderness areas. Their surprise attacks greatly frightened the people they looted. What angered the settlers most, though, was when the Beothuk cut away whole new salmon nets, or set moored boats adrift. Things came to a head in September 1818 when John Peyton Jr., Peyton Sr.'s son, lost a boat from his wharf on Sandy Point in the Bay of Exploits. He had been waiting for daybreak, for the next day's turn of the tide to take its valuable cargo to market. The boat was laden with salmon and furs, but there were also personal things aboard, such as clothes and bedding, silver watches, guns, pistols, ammunition, and cooking utensils. He had felt deeply uneasy all evening, and ordered his crew to keep watch until midnight. They then turned in so that they would be fresh for an early start.

What he did not realize, although he intuitively felt it, was that a Beothuk raiding party had been observing the household's movements for several days from a tall birch tree on a ridge behind the house. When he inspected the wharf once more before going to bed, the raiders were actually hidden in their canoe right beneath him, sitting so still and quiet that he failed to notice them. After a restless night, he came out in the early hours only to discover that his boat was gone. Nothing could be done until daybreak when an intensive search was launched. Peyton's boat was eventually discovered on the other side of the bay in a small creek at the mouth of Charles Brook. Everything portable was gone, including the cordage and sails, but the cargo was not damaged. The guns were found nearby, in the mud at the bottom of the brook, smashed and useless.

John Peyton Jr.'s patience broke. He went to St John's seeking permission from the now-presiding Governor Hamilton to travel into Beothuk territory to recover his stolen property. He also expressed the "most anxious desire" to capture one of the Red Indians alive and take the individual back to St John's. He may have felt that the £100 reward, which was still outstanding, would compensate for the expense of recovering his property. In any case, he was encouraged in his mission by the governor who, at the same time, insisted that there was to be no violence.

John Peyton Jr. left Sandy Point on March 1, 1819, with a party of eight furriers and his father, John Peyton Sr. He reiterated that no one was to open hostilities, unless he himself expressly ordered it. However, the party was well armed. Each man carried a musket, a bayonet, and a hatchet. Peyton Jr. had two pistols, a dagger, and a double-barreled gun (instead of a musket). They began by trekking up the Exploits River, and found several recently used campsites. There were five of Peyton's stolen marten traps and the jib of his plundered boat in one of the Beothuk storehouses. These finds spurred the men on. After five days of steady travel overland they arrived, on March 5, 1819, at the northeast arm of Red Indian Lake.

There are several versions of the dreadful events that happened next, but it seems that when they arrived at the lake a couple of the furriers took pot shots at some passing caribou. This alarmed the Beothuk. Men, women, and children swarmed out of three mammateeks and began to run off across the ice. The last stragglers were two men and a woman (whose name was later discovered to be Demasduit). She looked weak and ill and was carrying a baby in her arms. When she could not keep up, she handed the child over to one of the Beothuk men. At this moment, John Peyton Jr. sprinted forward. He threw off his snowshoes, jacket, and gun for greater speed, and managed to grab hold of her. She fell on her knees and opened her garment to show him her breasts. He understood this to be an attempt to plead for his mercy. Shanawdithit, recalling these events eight years later, said that Demasduit had been married for four years without any signs of a pregnancy, and that her first child had recently been born. She added, with deep sadness, that the baby died within two days of its mother's capture.

In the terror of the moment Demasduit called out, and two Beothuk men, her husband and his brother, turned back to help her. Her husband (she later said his name was Nonosabusut and that he was a chief) strode towards the settlers with a spruce bough in his hand to indicate his peaceful intentions. A powerful-looking man, he walked regally amongst the armed group and argued long and vehemently for her release. Instead of letting Demasduit go, John Peyton Jr. held her away from Nonosabusut. Her hands had already been bound with a handkerchief. Nonosabusut, who spoke no English but seemed to know something of European customs, shook hands with several of the party, again trying to show his peaceable intention. Then he attempted to drag her back. When he was prevented from freeing her he became deeply upset and an altercation broke out. He pulled a hatchet from the folds of his clothing but was disarmed by Peyton's men. He then grasped hold of Peyton Jr., who shook him off.

At this point Peyton Jr. began to drag the captured woman towards one of the mammateeks, trying to explain, through gestures, that she must go with him. He tried to indicate that her husband could go too, and that they would both be allowed to return to their people after a while. In desperation, Nonosabusut tried to wrestle the guns from several of the men near him. He failed, but struck two of them down, and managed to grab Peyton Sr. by the throat. The old man screamed out, "Are you going to stand by and let the Indian kill me?" In response, one trapper shot Nonosabusut, another stabbed him in the back with a bayonet, and others clubbed him with the butts of their muskets. Nonosabusut fell to the ice, bleeding from his mouth and nose, and died before his horrified wife's eyes. A witness later said that as he lay on the ice, "his eyes flashed fire and he uttered a yell that made the woods echo."

Meanwhile, the second Beothuk fled the scene. Shanawdithit, who was present throughout the incident, later related that he was Nonosabusut's brother and that he too, had been killed. The English party, who claimed that they had killed only one man, and that it was solely in self-defense, never admitted this. They reiterated that they had fired over the heads of the Beothuk to force them back, and that most of them had scattered.

The furriers took it all in a day's work, commenting on Nonosabusut's incredible height and his powerful physique. They made a callous show of measuring him for posterity's sake, declaring him to be 1.83 metres (well over six feet tall). More likely, they did this to boost their egos, to prove to all

that they had overcome an immensely powerful and dangerous opponent. The men covered the body with boughs. When
they forced the young woman away she broke down in grief,
and allowed them to take her to a nearby mammateek, where
the party spent the night. It was decided that they would
take her back to St John's, claim the reward, and use her to
establish friendly relations with her tribe. Given the circumstances surrounding her capture, this appears to have been
a ludicrous plan.

When the party returned, John Peyton Jr. was brought
before a grand jury at St John's to face an inquiry into the
murder. The jury found him not guilty. In summing up, the
judge remarked:

> *The deceased came to his death in consequence of*
> *an attack upon the party in search of them, and his*
> *subsequent obstinacy in not desisting when repeat-*
> *edly menaced by some of the party ... resulted in a*
> *merited death.*

After a further inquiry at Twillingate to corroborate the
evidence, Governor Hamilton reported that the party was
justified in acting as they did. His own official version of what
happened differed considerably from others. He wrote that
the furriers met a group of Beothuk who all ran away except
for one woman, "who exchanged friendly gestures." He went
on to say that others, who were not so friendly, approached

in increasing numbers, that they "laid hands" on Peyton's men, and that there was a struggle. Further, Hamilton wrote, when John Peyton Sr.'s life appeared to be in imminent danger, "one of the Beothuk fell to a musket ball." And, at that point, according to the governor, the Beothuk moved off and the trappers returned home accompanied, willingly, by the woman.

In fact, the young woman was far from compliant. Demasduit waited until her captors were asleep, then escaped by crawling away in the snow. In order to obliterate her tracks, she dragged her outer robe behind her. She had gone a fair distance when her absence was discovered and she was recaptured. Disheartened, Demasduit made no further attempts to escape, but stayed close to John Peyton Jr., appealing to him for protection. When she realized that she had no choice but to accompany the men, she settled herself in the sled (which was drawn in turn by one of four dogs), signalling the men to cover her and to lace her moccasins. This profoundly impressed them. The men were convinced that she was a person of consequence within her tribe, and that she was used to small niceties and to being waited on.

Shanawdithit later described the scene in great detail, illustrating the event with maps and drawings. She explained how desperately afraid the Beothuk were when they saw the nine heavily armed Englishmen approach the camp. They were sure that some of them would be taken to the coast and carried away on the ships, as so many of their ancestors

A portrait of Demasduit (renamed Mary March by her captors),
painted by Lady Henrietta Martha Hamilton in 1819.

had been in the past. As it was, Demasduit was conveyed to
the coast, but to Twillingate, not to a ship. She was placed in
the household of the Reverend John Leigh. This missionary
strongly believed the best way to raise "Red Indians" from a
state of "darkness and wildness" was to capture two young
boys (preferably between 12 and 18 years of age) and to

indoctrinate them for two or three years, then release them back into their community. The reverend stated that he knew of two people who were willing to take 10 or 12 of them in the summer "by mild means" at the rate of £100 per head.

Demasduit was placed under this radical man's care as soon as she reached Twillingate. The women who were selected to take care of her immediately scrubbed her clean of "red mud" and dressed her in English clothes. She refused to part with her own clothes, but did not try to wear them. Her complexion was approvingly deemed to be "nearly as fair as [a] European's after a course of washing and absence from smoke." She was also re-named by the English settlers and became known to them as Mary March (after the month in which she was captured).

At first Demasduit was deeply unhappy, and twice tried to escape into the woods, but after several weeks of careful watching she seemed to accept her new life. She was later remembered as having a great sense of humour. Prior to her ability to describe people by name, she would playfully mimic their profession or appearance. She especially enjoyed miming a shoemaker, a tailor, a blacksmith, or a man who wore glasses, all of whom must have looked very different from anyone she had ever known. Her skill at mimicry and her quickness in learning English, eventually enabled Reverend Leigh to compile a vocabulary of 180 words of the Beothuk language. Her captors reported that she did not eat much and did not like spirits. Part of the plan to befriend the

Beothuk was to introduce them to alcohol. No one seemed to be conscious of the fact that English food was foreign to the Beothuk. It was simply taken for granted that Demasduit would prefer it.

Reverend Leigh faulted her for sleeping too long. He also said that she was quite obstinate, and complained that she was only of help when it was not demanded of her. Throughout her stay with him, she was always planning for her return to her people. Demasduit told the reverend that 16 people lived in her mammateek. She regularly divided things she was given in captivity, such as trinkets, into 16 piles. She once hid some blue cloth in her room, and secretly sewed it into 16 pairs of moccasins.

When the ice broke up at Twillingate, Reverend Leigh took Demasduit for a short visit to St John's, where she charmed everyone who met her, including Governor Hamilton and his wife Lady Hamilton. Her modesty and intelligence were much admired. Lady Hamilton painted a miniature portrait of her and she was given many gifts. People began to revise their opinion of the Beothuk once they met Demasduit. An article in the *Mercantile Journal* of May 27, 1819, contrasts the notion of a savage and hostile Red Indian with the reality of the gentle and vibrant Demasduit, "Is it not horrible to reflect ... that many of her countrymen, in all probability as amiable and interesting as this young woman, are exposed to wanton cruelty ...."

Because of the love and concern Demasduit inspired,

a public meeting was called in St John's, where it was unanimously decided to return her to her people as soon as possible. A committee of six prominent citizens was elected to organize an expedition for the approaching winter, and a generous sum of money was raised on the spot. They decided that 30 men accustomed to the rough travel of the interior would accompany her to the Beothuk winter camp at Red Indian Lake. Until the departure, Demasduit would return to Twillingate, to be schooled in English by a selected tutor. Governor Hamilton was concerned about the initiative shown by this committee, one that was, essentially, beyond government control. He accordingly assigned Captain Glascock, commander of the HMS *Sir Francis Drake*, to the duty of sailing with Demasduit around the coastal settlements. The *Sir Francis Drake* was loaded with gifts for the anticipated reunion. Among them were tartan caps, sewing needles, sail needles, and various tools. In addition, there were soaps, tin kettles, dishes, small looking-glasses, and beads. Butter, tea, cheese, and sugar, which were unfamiliar to the Beothuk, were also included along with assorted domestic pottery.

When the *Sir Francis Drake* sailed into Twillingate Harbour, Captain Glascock fired two guns to signal Reverend Leigh to bring Demasduit on board. When she arrived, Captain Glascock was alarmed because she looked extremely fragile and ill. In fact, Demasduit was so emotionally and physically stressed that it was out of the question to expose her to travel in the small boats with the search parties. The captain made sure that she usually stayed on board. Captain Glascock, with John Peyton Jr. assisting him, diligently explored the coast around Fortune, the Exploits River as far as the lower falls, and the woods around Indian Bay and Badger Bay, all with no success. Eventually, at Seal Bay, they caught sight of a canoe, but Demasduit was unwilling to pursue it and stipulated that she would only rejoin the Beothuk if she was returned to the band she was taken from.

After the exciting chase of another canoe, which was foiled when a sailor fired a musket into the air, Glascock decided that his men were too exhausted to continue the search. He decided to take Demasduit back to Twillingate and then return to St John's. Disappointed at the failure of Glascock's mission, Governor Hamilton now appointed David Buchan, who had by this time gained the rank of captain, to take Glascock's place. He was told to make every effort to deliver Demasduit to her tribe at Red Indian Lake.

At the end of November 1819, John Peyton Jr. escorted Demasduit on board for her second reconnaissance trip, this time on the HMS *Grasshopper* at Twillingate (which Captain Buchan now commanded). Buchan was alarmed to see how rapidly her health had declined since he had last seen her in August. He supplied her with extra warm clothing, arranged for a woman to travel with her to take care of her needs, and he put her under the close supervision of the ship's surgeon. It was becoming painfully obvious that Demasduit would never be able to make the arduous trip on foot overland to

Red Indian Lake. Captain Buchan planned, instead, to make the trip himself and try to bring some of her people back to the ship to escort her home. Demasduit herself was firmly convinced that the Beothuk had moved away from that area. All she wished for now was to be re-united with her child — and to return to Twillingate (Demasduit was unaware the child had died shortly after her capture).

Unfortunately, on January 8, 1820, Demasduit died of consumption (tuberculosis). In her last few words she asked for John Peyton Jr., to whom she had grown attached. Her death caused considerable grief for those who had known and loved her. Both during her captivity and through her painful illness, her gentleness and patience had endured and had endeared her to others. It was now Captain David Buchan's painful task to deliver her remains to her people. He fitted out 49 men for the trip, which was expected to last 40 days. As well as food, the party carried 170 litres of rum. Their supplies and the presents for the Beothuk filled 12 sledges and several catamarans. They travelled heavily armed, with muskets, pistols, and pole-axes.

The party was delayed until the last week of January by a treacherous thaw. Most of the sledges, 8 of the 12, were badly damaged, and 14 men were sent back suffering from frostbite. Not until February 11 did they reach the area of Red Indian Lake from where Demasduit had been abducted. Only the frames of two of the three mammateeks were still intact. The third had been turned into a burial hut that contained the bodies of a large man and a child. The party believed that these must be the remains of Demasduit's husband, Nonosabusut and their child. Although Demasduit's coffin had been hauled over very rough country, it was still in good condition. It was covered with a fine red cloth, which was ornamented with copper trimming. Demasduit's body was decorated with gifts of trinkets, which she had received in captivity, and was still so unchanged that she seemed to the men almost alive. Captain Buchan ordered that the coffin be contained within a tent to keep it out of the reach of wild animals. The tent was ostentatiously draped with a Union Jack. Demasduit's coat and two wooden dolls, which she had treasured, were placed beside her.

Even though Buchan's men were exhausted and sick and were short of provisions, the party continued to search for the tribe. Here and there they left presents, with red flags attached to draw attention to them. These included iron spears made by the ship's armourer. Towards the end of the trip back, Captain Buchan sent most of the men back to the ship. He kept two men who were assigned to help him and John Peyton Jr. (who had accompanied the expedition), to explore inland from New Bay for another three days. They found only old traces of the tribe, and arrived back at the *Grasshopper* extremely fatigued, after a journey of 40 days. After several additional attempts, all of them unsuccessful, Captain Buchan returned to St John's to await further orders, still hopeful that one day his search would be rewarded.

It was still assumed that the Beothuk could be numbered in the hundreds. In fact there were only about 27 left by 1820. Eight years later, Shanawdithit produced accurate drawings depicting the exact course of Buchan's expedition, where he had left the coffin, and where his party had camped, both on the route inland and back to the ship. Although Buchan did not realize it at the time, the Beothuk had closely followed behind him marking his every move, all the while remaining carefully hidden. After the Beothuk confirmed that Buchan and his party had left the area and boarded the ship, they returned to where Demasduit's coffin had been left at Red Indian Lake. In the spring, the Beothuk conducted their sacred rites and moved her remains to lie beside that of her husband.

Nonosabusut's murder, Demasduit's capture, the death of their infant, and the trauma of the successive events, had all taken place during the course of less than 10 months.

Chapter 6
The Last Killing and Shanawdithit's Capture

Two years before Shanawdithit and her mother and sister were taken captive, a young man entered the scene. His dynamic energy, curiosity, and humanitarian interest were to bring the Beothuk question to the forefront of public consciousness in a way it never had been before.

William Eppes Cormack was born in Newfoundland in 1795, but by the time he was nine his family had moved back to Scotland, where his father had merchant interests. William Cormack went on to study natural sciences at the universities of Glasgow and Edinburgh. There he came under the mentorship of Professor Robert Jameson, founder of the Edinburgh Museum and editor of the *Edinburgh Philosophical Journal*.

His personal relationship with Professor Jameson, and his strong desire to impress him, was the driving force behind what became his obsessive interest in the Beothuk.

Cormack was a complex mix, both a humanitarian and a scientist. Not only did he believe the tribe to be on the verge of extinction, but also the scientist in him was convinced that they were a unique species of primitive mankind that would electrify the scientific world. When he returned to Newfoundland in 1821 to deal with family business, the tragic story of Demasduit and her enchanting personality was still fresh in people's minds and imaginations. Since her death in 1820, the Beothuk no longer appeared to the more sophisticated public of St John's as a stereotype of savagery. In a curious way, after years of expeditions to win the trust of the Native peoples, this charming young Beothuk woman turned it around so that she had, instead, won the trust of the English.

Cormack immediately became caught up in the flurry to reach the last of what was now more often thought of as this "noble and persecuted race." He believed that a small party of one or two people might have more chance of winning their confidence than a heavily armed expedition. William Cormack and Joseph Sylvester, a Mi'kmaq guide, set out from Random Bar on September 5, 1822, to walk due west across unexplored terrain to Bay St George. From the beginning, his Mi'kmaq guide was extremely nervous about crossing into Red Indian territory. Settlers at Bonaventure Bay who had tried to dissuade them at the start of the trip aggravated both men's fears. They were earnestly advised that the whole idea was hazardous and foolhardy. Besides, said the settlers, they had no idea of the rough conditions in the interior. They would be killed by wolves or attacked by murderous Red Indians or die of starvation. The trouble was that the thought of all of these realistic obstacles affected Cormack's frame of mind. He later wrote that he lay awake at night oppressed by thoughts "of no ordinary kind," in contrast to the nighttime thoughts of his guide who, being quite used to the wilderness, slept soundly. Walking was arduous. Between them they carried a heavy load of camp gear: a telescope, compasses, and 33 pounds of food, as well as fishing equipment and guns. They pushed through dense woods, and across wilderness and barrens. Mosquitoes and myriad other insects constantly tormented them.

As the mild fall gave way to winter, the nights became very cold. Snowstorms made it difficult to keep going, and there was no dry ground to sleep on, or dry wood for a fire. Their food gave out, and they had to hunt to survive. They were often starving and dangerously exhausted. Cormack worried that his strength would fail him, but he was buoyed by the thought that they were passing through Beothuk country. In fact they weren't. Still feeling apprehensive at the thought of encountering Red Indians, his Mi'kmaq guide deliberately misled them to the south, into Mi'kmaq territory. They did, however, meet up with wolves as predicted, but even these refused to spice up their adventure, and simply fled at their approach. After two months fearful privation, they staggered into St George's on November 2, 1822. Cormack was bitterly disappointed at finding no trace of the Beothuk. When Cormack was sufficiently recovered, he amazingly set out alone on the 322-kilometre journey on foot and by sea to Fortune, where he caught a ship back to England.

Only two months after the termination of Cormack's desperate search for signs of the tribe, two weak and starving Beothuk, a man and his daughter, stumbled out of the woods begging for help. Two furriers, James Carey and Stephen Adams — without a moment's hesitation — gunned them down. Months later, on June 23, 1823, Carey and Adams were tried in St John's for manslaughter. James Carey claimed self-defence. He testified that he and his partner were terrified when the pair rushed towards them brandishing knives. The knives (if they existed) were never brought before the court as evidence. Chief Justice Tucker, whose sympathies clearly lay with the furriers, instructed the jury. He advised them that if a man could be proved to have acted out of fear for his own safety, then homicide was justifiable. He included a long list of "Red Indian atrocities" in order to drive home his point. When several credible witnesses emphasized the danger and risk that furriers faced, both men were exonerated. No one cared to defend the Beothuk formally, even though there was increasing public concern about their plight.

And two months before the trial of Steven Adams and

James Carey took place, and before their part in the murders had come to light in April 1823, a small party of trappers from the Twillingate area bent forward eagerly, tracking prints in the snow at Badger Bay ....

Once again, the same James Carey (the self-proclaimed Indian killer) was on the hunt. "Red Indians, probably women," he noted with satisfaction. The pattern of the snowshoes was unmistakable. It was close to this area that he and Stephen Adams had snuffed out the lives of a man and woman only weeks ago. Just as well to keep quiet about it, though ... settlers were getting increasingly lily-livered about dealing with these vermin. To Carey's mind, killing the "savages" had not been murder but good riddance. Two less to pilfer his traps and fishing nets, or to vandalize the boats. He would teach these "heathens" not to ruin his business. This was his territory to hunt and fish in any way he wished. Let no one mistake it!

James Carey and Stephen Adams had linked forces with William Cull and some other furriers for this particular tracking expedition. The snow made it easy to pick up a continuous trail, and about 10 kilometres from Carey's house the group came upon a single mammateek. As they approached they thought they saw a man slip away. The trackers gathered together to discuss the situation, wary of possible unwelcome surprises. Were there others around? The first thing to do was to test out the mammateek. They charged through the skins that draped the entrance, muskets and pistols at the ready.

There was only an old woman inside, crouched on the floor, looking horrified and bewildered. They wrenched her to her feet. As they did so she was wracked with a spluttering cough, and they backed off, disgusted. They might as well take her though, and collect the government reward of £100 for the capture of a Beothuk. It was a considerable sum of money ... and easy to earn in this case. She seemed a relatively harmless old hag, other than her disgusting cough ... not likely to give much trouble on the way back.

The furriers took her to the local justice of the peace, John Peyton Jr., first. This man was, by this time, well known for his claim to want reconciliation with the Beothuk tribe. Not that he and his father hadn't given the Red Indians plenty to worry about in the past. When the party reached the Peyton household, the old woman looked around with a look of sheer hatred on her lined face. She knew very well where she was and the sort of men who lived here. The old man especially, Peyton Sr., was a stalker and a sadistic killer, diabolically patient in planning attacks against her people. Not just once, but over many years, again and again. And he showed no mercy.

That son of his, John Peyton Jr., despite his claims of friendship with the tribe, also had a dark side. He had led a party of armed men to their camp at Red Indian Lake five years earlier to recover stolen property. He had taken hostage one of their young women. But first — he savagely killed her husband Nonosabusut — right before her eyes. The old woman shrank at the dreadful but still-vivid memory, and recalled that Demasduit's lifeless body had been furtively returned to the deserted Beothuk camp months later, and hidden in the forest inside a wooden box. It had been shrouded with the wicked soulless trappings of the English. This same man she remembered from that day now appraised her, thoughtfully. John Peyton Jr. was aware of her anger, and its cause. There was no benefit to him to house this sick old Beothuk woman in his place overnight, he reckoned. For one thing, he did not want to attract a possible Red Indian rescue attempt. For another, she was filthy as well as vehemently angry. Besides ... he had only recently brought home his sweet 17-year-old bride, Eleanor. Why expose her to unnecessary danger or fear? Why force her to deal with such an unpleasant "guest"?

Peyton instructed Cull, one of his employees, to take her in for the night. But the snow was driving hard and there were enormous drifts. Thus, the party was forced to put up at the house of another man at Indian Point instead. The old woman was so weak that one of the kindlier men supported her the last part of the way. He was appalled by how thin she was under her bulky skin robes. "No wonder she can scarcely walk, this old [body] is starved," he said, as he gave her into the care of the women of the household. But when they offered her food, she was unable to eat any of the salt meat they pressed upon her. Unaccustomed to the food, her stomach immediately rejected it. In addition, her gut-tearing cough made her constantly retch, and it was hard for her to swallow.

The search for the other two women, whose footprints they had seen, started as soon as the bitter weather let up a little. This was an exceptionally cold winter, and the going was rough. It took the men two weeks of careful tracking, and when they found them, it was almost by accident. Very young, scarcely more than girls really, they were squatting in a mammateek over a feeble fire, shaking with the cold, and clearly in an advanced stage of starvation. They were too weak to hunt for even small game, and had subsisted on the few handfuls of mussels they had gathered from the rocks along the shore. They were now so dulled by hunger, exhaustion, and cold that they surrendered themselves to the furriers without any resistance at all. The men tried to let them know through signs that the old lady had been captured. They seemed to understand, and wearily resigned themselves to the daunting trek back through wilderness country ....

The two girls were taken in triumph to John Peyton Jr.'s house. No one had realized that the older woman was their mother until they greeted each other with obvious relief. The sisters told their mother that their father now lay dead. Shortly after the trappers had caught a glimpse of him outside the mammateek, he had tried to escape by crossing a creek. He had fallen through weak ice and drowned. When others of the tribe realized he could not be saved, they had pushed off deeper into the forest. However, the sisters stayed behind and remained in the area. None of the three captives gave any sign that they were in mourning, or that they were terrified. They exercised a stoic control in the presence of their enemies. At any rate, few settlers would have been prepared to give the women's feelings much thought. These Native women were of a different species after all (thought the settlers), and almost certainly did not have the same capacity for emotion as white people.

First things first. Certainly the "savages" must be thoroughly scrubbed before they could even be brought into the same room with polite society. Not only were they filthy from their journey through the bush, but their skin, hair, and clothes were saturated with layer upon layer of red-coloured grease. And they were rank. The zinc bath was pulled down from where it hung from a nail on the scullery wall and dragged in front of the kitchen stove, where it was filled with kettle after kettle of steaming water. Several worthy wives gathered around, and set to with a will to scour the women clean. The strong lye soap did the trick in the end, but it was hard labour to get the results they needed. For one thing they had to subdue each of the women in turn, as all three put up a strong resistance. It never occurred to anyone that the ochre was anything but dirt.

Even years later, when the youngest girl, Shanawdithit, learned to speak a little English, she could never share the spiritual violation she must have felt during this experience. Deeply modest, not only were they stripped naked and forced to endure the rude curious stares and the mocking remarks of these pale females, but they were despoiled of their distinctive tribal markings. No one realized that the red ochre symbolized initiation into the community in infancy, or that it was renewed annually throughout one's lifetime when the tribe gathered together for the caribou hunt. The settlers did not know that these ceremonies were occasions for solemn reflection, dancing, and rejoicing, or that the ochre was only removed as a punishment for having incurred the wrath of the tribe for a serious offence, such as fraternization with an enemy. For the Beothuk women, the scrubbing experience aroused frightening and complex feelings of ostracism and guilt, and they were powerless under the roof of their captors.

Finally, the Englishwomen stood back from their work around the bath, satisfied. The "savages" were pronounced clean. Now it was time to outfit them from head to toe in English clothing. They produced bonnets, shoes, and stockings, and fitted them with care. Hardly an inch of skin was left exposed. Now they were dressed like civilized folk, as they should be. Only one last detail remained. The revolting deerskin robes must be burned in the stove. They met more than their match in this, though. The three women fiercely resisted every attempt to wrest their garments away, clutching the robes desperately against their breasts. In the end it was easier to let them have their way, rather than tear their new outfits in an unseemly struggle. Surely it would be possible to sneak them away later. It wasn't. The three Beothuk women stubbornly carried the deerskin robes everywhere, adamantly refusing to be parted from them for any reason. What the English women had no inkling of was the sacredness of personal clothing among many Native peoples. Clothing was not just functional and decorative, but an innate part of a person's identity. Garments were an extension of the spirit. It was taboo to allow even a close friend to wear one's clothes. Should an enemy gain possession of them, they would surely use the clothing to put a curse on the owner. The Beothuk women, who believed that white people harboured an evil spirit, were placed in an agonizing dilemma. The experience of wearing their enemies' dress, even if involuntarily, was a terrifying ordeal.

It was now time to give the captives proper Christian names. It was not necessary to try to find out what they were called in their own language, they would have to learn English as soon as possible anyway. The easiest thing to do was to name the women with some reference to their capture. This was what had always been done in the past. The elder sister would be called Easter Eve, after the season. The younger girl, (Shanawdithit) was renamed Nancy April, after the month she was captured. Their mother came to be known by the English as Betty Decker, because the men who took her were decking a boat at the time. She was also given the insulting nick-name of Old Smut, because she had such a dark scowling expression that the settlers believed her capable of cruel and wicked deeds.

Since it was constantly in the forefront of the settlers' minds that the capture of the three women could very well result in a substantial government reward, it was agreed that the women should be transferred as soon as possible to St John's and put into the hands of the governor. As well, John Peyton Jr. wanted to ensure that they would not be exposed to undue danger at Sandy Point, as there was an undercurrent of anti-Native sentiment among the settlers around the Exploits River area that had erupted in the past into vicious murders. Peyton's new schooner, the *Anne,* had just been launched at his shipyard in Lower Sandy Point, and he planned to sail it to St John's himself.

The women were extremely frightened when they understood that they were to be taken on board a ship. The warnings that had been instilled in them from birth now filled them with dread. No Beothuk had ever been known to return from a sailing vessel. They also had anxieties about being held responsible for tribal acts of war. The women were sure that Peyton Jr. did not know about their part in the theft of his personal property in the past, but it hardly mattered. He knew they were from the same tribe. The mother and her two daughters were distraught. What fate awaited them at sea at the mercy of this vengeful man? Where were they going? Were they about to be punished for past crimes of killing and theft that had never been forgotten? All that they could do was comfort each other and hope that they would be allowed to remain together.

The *Anne* docked at St John's on June 18. The fact that Captain David Buchan was acting governor in Hamilton's absence in England was fortunate for the captive women. Buchan cared deeply about the plight of their people, and had been in charge of many unsuccessful and tragic attempts to contact the tribe. Captain Buchan expressed grave concern about the health of all three. He was especially apprehensive over the state of Easter Eve, who appeared to have an advanced case of tuberculosis. Captain Buchan thought it likely that the other two were infected, as well. All three were severely undernourished and looked very ill. He asked the surgeon of the HMS *Grasshopper*, which was under his command, to physically examine them. The physician decided that Easter Eve, in particular, should be bled.

Bleeding (also known as blood-letting or phlebotomy) was the preferred medical treatment of the time for all kinds of sickness. It was believed that the procedure released ill humours (toxins) from the body, and relieved pressure on the circulatory system. However, it was a frightening process for someone who had never seen it before. It involved the surgeon opening a vein with a sharp knife and allowing as much blood to flow as he felt was appropriate for the disease and the strength of the patient. The surgeon was deeply concerned that none of the women would have any idea of what he was attempting to do. Since he could not use language to explain himself, he decided to demonstrate on a volunteer first. He completed his grisly demonstration, and then suddenly advanced towards the elder girl with the knife, clearly intent on slicing her vein open next. Betty Decker and Shanawdithit rushed to Easter Eve and threw their arms around her protectively, shrieking and striking out like wildcats. There was no way the surgeon could have got his knife near any of them. They made such a commotion that he gave up on the idea entirely, embarrassed at how the noise might be interpreted. It is not difficult to imagine what it must have looked like to the women. They were aboard a heavily armed naval ship and they knew they were prisoners of war, and they also knew that their own tribe often ceremoniously executed prisoners by beheading.

Meanwhile Captain David Buchan asked the high sheriff to find them comfortable and safe quarters where crowds would not molest them. He put them up in furnished rooms in the courthouse, in the main area of town. This was the first time any of them had slept inside a stone building, and the cold, impenetrable walls must have given them a sense of claustrophobia and imprisonment, rather than the safety and comfort that was intended. They were used to the filtered light and fresh smell of sap in a closed mammateek. In this room there was little feeling of privacy. When they looked out of the great windows, they could see they were surrounded on all sides by buildings, and feared the prying eyes of townspeople. The old woman crouched all day on the floor, wearing her deerskin robe like a shawl over her English clothing. She glared around defiantly, hating being on display.

They were given no choice over the visitors they received. And they were soon invaded by two critical Methodist clergymen, Reverend Wilson from Grand Bank and Reverend Ellis from Burin. The Reverend Wilson was highly judgemental about the captives sleeping on their deerskins in the corner. To ignore the beds, he felt, signified primitive, barely human, origins. In fact the women found solace and comfort in this. In their mammateeks they always slept crowded together in a circle around a central hearth.

Every aspect of English habits of personal hygiene and toiletry was unfamiliar and bizarre to the captives. Even the fastenings of their clothes were strange and intimidating. Food they could not eat was dished up on hard plates on a table, and they were given cutlery to eat it with, which they had no idea how to use. They craved the sweet-smelling birchbark containers of home. Using their fingers, they ate sparingly, swallowing just enough to keep up their strength.

Despite the discomfort, the exuberant Shanawdithit enjoyed experimenting with her novel surroundings. Shanawdithit seemed to have great fun grimacing into the looking glass, and Reverend Wilson was fascinated by the way she amused herself with the tick of his watch. But what really amazed him was her aptitude for drawing. He later wrote to the Methodist Missionary Society that when given a lead pencil and a piece of paper, she "made a few marks on the paper apparently to try the pencil; then in one flourish she drew a deer perfectly, starting at the tip of its tail." Five years down the road this would be remembered, and her drawings would become a means of conveying what she

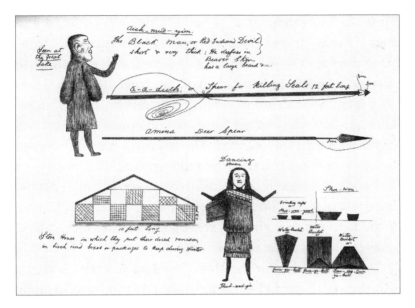

Drawings by Shanawdithit

could express of her culture. For now the two ministers were gratified that they could observe enough intelligence among the trio to warrant their making an effort to convert these heathen beings to Christianity.

The hostages were soon allowed to walk openly down the street, and wherever they went gawking onlookers surrounded them. St John's was a bustling garrison town with a settled population of over 10,000, as well as a huge swell of seasonal fishermen and merchants. Shanawdithit appeared amused by the curiosity of the children in the crowd and, from time to time, she darted out mischievously and pretended to catch some of them. When they scattered in fright, she went into peals of unrestrained mirth and thoroughly enjoyed their dismay. They were wearing the English dresses, but all three insisted on draping their deerskin cloaks over them. Shanawdithit had torn off the brim of her English bonnet and decorated her forehead and arms with tinsel and coloured paper. Government officials invited them to select whatever they wished from neighbourhood shops. They were astounded to see such a profusion of goods, and after choosing a few pieces of inexpensive jewellry for themselves, they loaded their arms with pots, kettles, hatchets, hammers, and nails (all highly prized by the Beothuk).

Nevertheless, for the three Beothuk women, St John's was the very heart of hostile territory, and they walked along the streets of their enemies like alien beings with their bodies crammed into tight, uncomfortable foreign clothes, their spirits challenged to the utmost. They experienced firsthand the awesome extent of the white invasion and truly had their fill of it.

They hugged their deerskins closely around them, to fend off the chill wind and hide their shameful English clothes. Raising their sorrowful faces towards the hills where their ancestors had once thrived, they wondered what to expect next.

Chapter 7
The Attempted Return of Shanawdithit to Her People

Captain Buchan was most anxious to get the women back as soon as possible to their own people, and it was his strong hope that they would return with good feelings about their "visit." His greatest concern was that Easter Eve was obviously failing. If she died on their hands it would look as if the English had killed her, or at least neglected her to a criminal extent. Far from reassuring the tribe, it would reinforce implacable attitudes of hatred.

They would carry with them the load of gifts and utensils that were intended to show how well they were treated. They were encouraged to resume their native dress. Being forced to wear English clothes was obviously a sore point with them, rather than a privilege. Buchan also tried to impress on the three women that, should they ever be in trouble, they could rely on the kindness of white people, especially officials like himself. This was difficult to convey convincingly because of the long history of cruelty and mistrust on both sides, but he thought that perhaps the young girl, Shanawdithit, might at least partially believe him (as things turned out this proved to be true).

He arranged for John Peyton Jr. to transport them back to the area where they had been discovered. He also covered (through government funding) the expenses for their sea passage, their safe delivery overland to Charles Brook, and several days' supply of food to leave in the forest with them. In seeing to these details himself, he did his utmost to ensure their smooth return (which in fact was much more than most government officials were prepared to do, including Governor Hamilton when he returned from England.)

Once they got over the first of their fears and realized they were not about to be tortured or put to death, the Beothuk women were fascinated by the bustle around them. The two garrison forts, Fort William and Fort Townshend, were alive with the activities of armed soldiers coming and going. Around the outskirts of Fort William were dozens of small vegetable plots that were cultivated by both officers and men to eke out food supplies. The town of St John's was a blend of extreme wealth and extreme poverty. The Beothuk women were amazed at the frenzied pace of life, and rather afraid of it all. The paths immediately above the north side of the harbour led to wharves and fish stores, and to huge warehouses and storehouses. There, outgoing vessels could be re-stocked with provisions and goods, or display their own unloaded cargoes for sale. Streams and brooks that ran down the side of the hill overflowed and worsened the muddy narrow tracks, and the noisy crowds squelched through them with curses. Sea dogs, foreign fishermen, fishery servants, traders, fishing captains, pirates, jacky tars, and naval officers all elbowed for space with local residents for the chance to buy and barter. An alehouse was near at hand for a boisterous finish to the day's business.

The majority of streets were flanked by hovels and the burned-out shells of buildings that had been razed by the terrible fire of 1816. There was an overall feeling of squalor that was intensified by a pervading stench of fish and poor sanitation. The Beothuk women felt sickened. They had never been exposed to anything like it before. The tribe generally occupied a site for a relatively short time and moved on before refuse accumulated to an unhealthy level.

Signs of emerging wealth offset the sordid environment. Merchants and professionals had built some fine homes. These families rode through the unpaved tracks in carriages or horse and trap, employed female domestic servants, and patronized an increasing number of shops.

The Beothuk women were fascinated by all of these sights, which were entirely outside their experience. They gazed through the windows at the activities within the baker's, the glazier's, the barber's, the tailor's, and the watchmaker's shops. Shanawdithit was especially drawn to this last shop. Her experience of listening to the Reverend Wilson's watch that first day at the courthouse fired her imagination. She had seen similar gadgets in the cargoes of some of the boats the tribe had stolen, but the Beothuk had never understood what they were for and had been content to dismantle them and use the inner wheels and movements as ornaments or as spiritual symbols.

The Beothuk women were also astounded to observe the newly established local fire brigade at work on a burning wooden building. Scores of townsfolk joined in to sling leather buckets from hand to hand as they fought against time to douse the flames. Officious members of the recently formed constabulary kept people back. The captives were surprised to see that the leather buckets very much resembled the birchbark ones the Beothuk made.

The three women stayed in the town of St John's for 10 days. On June 28th the *Anne* was ready for departure, and they were given a kind farewell by Captain Buchan and other people who had taken an interest in their welfare. Their gifts were carefully packed and loaded with them, but when they took the small open boat out to the schooner, they still had no idea where they were going. They were numbed by the cold wind off the grey Atlantic waves, and shaken by paroxysms of coughing. The coughs of each one of them had grown worse from their stay in the dark, damp rooms of the courthouse. They rowed past the vast numbers of sailing ships that crowded the sheltered waters. The sides of the ships bristled with guns for the defence of the warlike fishing fleets. Overhead wheeled millions of screaming sea birds, attracted to the fish offal that was thrown off the ships, and to the bloody decks.

Their last view of the settlement was of the fishermen's homes at Quidi Vidi, clustered at the foot of the towering cliffs of Signal Hill, and of the battery cannons that had been mounted 200 years before to fight off pirates. Then they were through the Narrows and leaving behind them the new lighthouse of Fort Amherst, at the entrance to the harbour. They had watched its bright glare at night from their windows, and it had been a constant reminder of their vulnerability in the grip of overwhelming power and engineering skill.

As the sails were furled, they had a flutter of hope. They were not headed for the open sea, but were hugging the coast. Once they neared Funk Island and the Exploits Bay they knew where they were, and gratefully sniffed the smell of trees, which was carried on the wind offshore. It was fragrant with reminders of their own people. When they reached the Peyton household at Lower Sandy Point, they were given a small hut outside the main house and supplied with food. Although they were still clearly captives, they had a little more independence and privacy.

As Easter Eve's cough worsened again, her mother became increasingly concerned. It was obvious to her that the girl was dying. Together the three of them made a small shelter of boughs to create a sweat lodge. Large rocks were heaped outside the entrance and a fire lit under and around them until they were scorching hot. The three entered the low structure on their knees, with the smell of the damp earth and resinous pine boughs reminding them of home. Solemnly Shanawdithit pried rocks from the fire and coaxed them into the centre of the sweat lodge. Leaning over the glowing rocks, the older woman sprinkled a little water, chanting. Clouds of scalding steam billowed throughout the tiny structure, raising the temperature to an almost unbearable level. Seeing the wisps of vapour escaping through the cracks, curious locals assumed that the medicine woman, as she was believed to be, had created a vapour bath to treat Easter Eve's sickness.

This was true, but only partially so. The sweat lodge was a sacred place for prayer and purification, as well as healing. As each glowing rock was settled ceremoniously in the centre, and water sprinkled once again, a new round of incantation and prayer began. Reverence was offered to ancestors and powerful guardian spirits. It was an opportunity to speak and listen from the soul, as well as to breathe in the healing, soothing clouds of vapour. This powerful connection with their own tradition helped to preserve their courage and give them the strength and hope to continue. It also helped prepare each one of them for death. They knew that their future was uncertain, and that every hour spent together in this sacred place was precious.

They had been held in captivity for about three months when John Peyton Jr. decided it was time to return them to the wilderness. The party set out in mid-July laden down with the gifts they had picked out at St John's. This large bundle of gifts was bulky and awkward to carry, and the men shouldered it as far as Charles Brook in Notre Dame Bay. They left the three women there with reassuring pats and smiles, wished them well in the search for their people, and provided them with enough bread, pork, and butter to last for a few days. They were also given a flat-bottomed boat and paddles to carry them downstream along the River Exploits, so that they could easily search both banks. The Beothuk were well known for hiding in unexpected and unrevealing places, and were difficult to spot at the best of times. Before he left, Peyton again encouraged them to return with friends once they had met up with the tribe, and Shanawdithit gave him the impression that she would try to do this, rewarding him with one of her vivacious glances. Little did either of them suspect how soon, and under what tragic circumstances, she would be back.

Then the party of men who had accompanied them rounded a bend in the river and they were on their own, surrounded by pots, pans, and wilderness. They would have been glad of their freedom, except that it was not the kind of situation they were used to in their former environment. They still could not digest European food easily, and that was all they were provided with. In the past they would have been properly equipped with light weapons to hunt small game, but they had not been given adequate equipment or tools for this part of their journey.

This was no time to worry about what reception they might receive from the tribe. They were all so sick that they did not have the strength to build an adequate shelter for the night. Exposed to the cold and damp, exhausted by the physical and emotional stress of the past months, the old woman became too weak to travel any farther. Her lungs filled up with tubercular phlegm and she collapsed, gasping for breath. The two girls gently covered her with her deerskin cloak, and each clung to a hand. Bending close to her withered cheeks, they whispered their love for her and prayed for protection on her journey to the afterworld. They assured her they would give her a proper burial, according to tradition, and she was greatly comforted. At the same time she was overcome with anguish about the new dangers her daughters would face. Their dying mother pleaded with the Creator to protect them, but soon all she was able to concentrate on was breathing. The sisters tried to ease her spasms of coughing, but there was little they could do for her, and within a few hours she died. They were alone in the forest.

Reverently, they stripped sheets of bark from surrounding birch trees and closely wrapped them around their mother's frail body. Between them, weak as they were, they managed to scratch out a shallow grave. They stayed beside their mother for a while, reluctant to let her go. They knew it was necessary to protect her body from marauding animals before nightfall, so they heaped the low mound with rocks, and committed her to the protection of Mother Earth.

The two sisters clung together until long after the moon topped the trees. Brokenhearted and exhausted, they rose early the next morning, said final prayers over their mother's grave, and unhitched the boat. They had talked things over during the night, and decided that it was too dangerous to stay in the forest. They would go back to Lower Sandy Point and ask one of the settler families for help. Shanawdithit paddled. Her sister was too weak to help. Prostrated by her gut-wrenching cough, it was all she could do to stay conscious. By the time they made it to the settlement, she had reached the limit of her endurance. Shanawdithit stopped at the nearest homestead, Cooper Pike's place. He was a kindly man, and very concerned when he recognized who they were. His wife settled the almost comatose Easter Eve in comfortably, but Shanawdithit was too anguished to relax. She paced up and down, grieving the loss of her mother and fearing for Easter Eve.

Within a week her sister's condition worsened, and she died in Shanawdithit's arms. She could not manage to prepare a birchbark shroud on her own, but she sewed her sister's body into a blanket and the men of the house saw

Shanawdithit, the last-known Beothuk of Newfoundland

to the burial. Shanawdithit stood by the shallow grave and dropped small pieces of birchbark upon her still form, completing what she could of the traditional rites. She prayed fervently for her sister's safe passage to the land of the ancestors, beyond the sunset. Now only I am left, she thought. Who will pray with me when it is my time to go on that dangerous journey? Will you meet me and guide me, my beloved sister?

Deeply troubled at being utterly alone, no tribe to support her, no family left, she thanked the Pikes and set off for the Peyton's place. John Peyton Jr. had told her, just before he had left them alone in the wilds, that he would always help her if she needed him. She untied the little flat bottomed boat from its mooring at the riverbank. They had accepted it with such hope just a short time ago. The river currents were strong, but Shanawdithit negotiated the dangerous waters with skill. Travelling alone gave her a desperate courage. Her fate was in her own hands and she knew she must do the unthinkable. She must surrender herself to the white-skinned ones once again. Shanawdithit had no clear vision for the future. In her anguish and grief, her mind was flooded with questions. The settlers had been so determined to return the three of them to their people that she did not know what to expect. For one thing, if the settlers did force her back to the wilderness, would she find herself cast out of the tribe? Would her people view her as a social pariah who had been contaminated by living among the hated English?

When Shanawdithit arrived back on the Peyton's doorstep, they too were faced with an unexpected dilemma. Who would take her in? There was enough anti-Native feeling in the community to make the situation awkward and possibly dangerous for anyone who did. Would she become the focus of Beothuk reprisal raids? But even if that did not happen, would she fit in to the life of a white household successfully? Shanawdithit had lived in captivity for a very short time. She had been taken in April and it was now August. Apart from the lodgings at the courthouse where everything was done for her, she was not used to living in a house, could not keep food down easily, and was unable to speak English. She was unlikely to be much help around the household as the colonists' style of living was completely foreign to her. They knew she was not yet civilized enough to use conventional furniture. And she was definitely not comfortable in English clothing.

Would Shanawdithit attempt to run away or perhaps act in rebellious ways, or even burn the house down in a fit of spite? The Beothuk had a long history of setting fire to tilts. She had no moral background or Christian training. What ideas would she transmit to any youngsters she might be thrown in with? Was she a thief? After all, the Beothuk had long been pilfering from local fishing stations and tilts. In reality, this young Indian girl was an unknown quantity and, by and large, an unwelcome one. It was one thing to collect a prize group of Indians for a reward, and groom them for a peace mission, but quite another to bring a single dirty vagabond permanently into one's home.

In the end, since no one else would take a chance with her, Peyton and his young bride accepted the responsibility. John Peyton did not ask government approval for assuming custody of her, but he did submit a bill, as agreed with Buchan, for her board and lodging between August 1 and October 16. He received payment of £51, which also covered the expenses he incurred transporting them all to and from

St John's, and then back to the wilderness. He never did receive the reward money for their capture. In any case, this particular mission could not be called a success. The prime purpose had been to establish goodwill between the English and the Beothuk. The end result was two dead and one — still little more than a youngster — left to fend for herself.

In taking the girl into his home Peyton was certainly taking a considerable risk, but it also enabled him to exercise some control over her. He knew that she had enough specific information about atrocities committed by his family and friends to cause considerable trouble for him once she learned to speak English. Much of his conduct in the past had been questionable. He had been brought to court to answer questions about the deaths of the Beothuk who had been slain during the supposedly peaceful expedition he had led to Red Indian Lake in 1819. In addition, he had testified for the defence at the trial of James Carey and Stephen Adams for the murder of Shanawdithit's uncle and cousin, and he had been a major influence in their acquittal.

Peyton's father, John Peyton Sr., who lived with them, was a notorious "Indian killer." At one time the magistrate for Bonavista had even recommended that Peyton Sr. be expelled from the Exploits area. Peyton Sr., he claimed, was infamous for his persecution of Native peoples: "The stories told of this man would shock humanity." And there was considerable irony in the fact that a series of events had resulted in bringing Shanawdithit and Peyton Sr. together under the same roof. Shanawdithit was aware that she would have to tread very carefully in this household.

The benefit for the Peyton family in keeping Shanawdithit was the opportunity to mend their tarnished reputation. In giving her a safe and kind refuge, John Jr. was able to publicly establish a humanitarian reputation, and show in a concrete way that he was now motivated to reach out to a wronged people. So, in spite of all the doubts and risks, Shanawdithit was absorbed into the Peytons' family life. However "uncivilized" she may have appeared initially, she was soon introduced to the skills of domestic servant and learned to speak in pidgin English. Before long she was able to tell the family that her real name was Shanawdithit (and some of the English settlers began to use her name instead of referring to her as Nancy April or Nance).

In fact, her Beothuk name seemed to give her some connection with her own reality. But she would never again meet up with anyone of her tribe, or be able to communicate fluently in her own language. Shanawdithit had no tribe and no family. The only thing she had left was her name.

Chapter 8

Shanawdithit Quietly Closes the Door on Her Past

Shanawdithit strove to control her tears. Only a short time had passed since she had stumbled through the storm with her sister to find that their mother was also a captive. She remembered how, when they told their mother that their father had drowned, their mother had demanded that they hold back their tears in front of the enemy. "Never show your wounds," she had said. "They are your weakest point — where you will most likely be attacked again."

In Shanawdithit's tiny room was a flyspecked mirror. Thinking back to the time she had first peered into a looking glass (when the three of them were still together at St John's), she once more grimaced at her reflection. Then she slowly discarded her beloved native dress. She carefully began the tedious business of buttoning on her European clothes again. When she had left those clothes behind to embark on her journey home, she had thought she was rid of them forever. She looked at her transformed reflection. "Your name is Shanawdithit," she whispered to it. "You are Shanawdithit. No one can take that from you." Then she slipped on her hard shoes in preparation for the road she must now tread alone, and quietly closed the door on her past ....

It was sometimes difficult to be cheerful and pleasant when no one understood her language, but Shanawdithit's easygoing personality was one of her greatest gifts. What struck people most about her was her boisterous spirit. Even when she was first captured she seemed irrepressible and overflowing with curiosity. But she also had a serious side. Dr. Carson wrote that she was "majestic, mild, and tractable, but characteristically proud and cautious." Shanawdithit now found herself living in the kind of settlement that was utterly abhorred by her people.

When Shanawdithit was taken in by the Peytons in 1823, she entered the household of successful and shrewd businessmen, who maintained their strong European connections. And despite their rough reputation, the family was highly respected. On the other hand, life in the outport was very raw. It was an extremely lawless part of the country. The authorities had little control over the wild settlers. Chief Justice Reeves complained, "people do as they like and there is hardly any time of account for their actions." Nevertheless, John Peyton Jr. had political aspirations. By 1818, five years prior to Shanawdithit's arrival in their home, Governor Hamilton had appointed John Peyton Jr. to the position of justice of the peace for northern Newfoundland.

Life in the outport was designed for survival in a fixed environment. Shanawdithit longed for the freedom of the forests and the rivers. She had spent her entire life on the move and it was difficult for her to adjust to a settled way of life in a permanent house. Earthen paths connected weather-beaten homes and garden patches that had been wrested from the forest, rather than remaining part of its life cycle. Shanawdithit had never experienced cultivated food before. She was surprised that settlers grew strange thick-skinned root vegetables, such as turnip, and whatever else proved tough enough to battle the short cold seasons. A few farm animals, which had made the traumatic Atlantic crossing by sailing ship, grazed here and there. Hens scratched around in the dirt, and she was woken every dawn by the unfamiliar crow of the cock. When she helped with the cows, she was constantly reminded of how much the cattle angered her people. The Beothuk deeply resented the encroachment on the forest to pasture them.

Shanawdithit had an unusual status within the household. At that time in history, it would not have been considered outrageous to treat her as a slave. There was a long history of Native peoples being taken into slavery throughout the North American continent. However, Shanawdithit was not treated as a slave, although she was expected to help with domestic work. But this work was on a fairly casual and often voluntary basis. John Peyton Jr. was convinced that she more or less did what she liked, and a male employee confirmed this. That was the opinion of the men. However, the other female domestic staff that worked alongside her remembered it differently. Two of them later recalled that she worked very hard, and more than pulled her weight in doing household chores. She made the fires, swept and scrubbed floors, washed clothes, prepared tea, and helped with the cooking and sewing, all of which were new tasks, if not new concepts, for her. She had to learn all these domestic chores from scratch, although she continued to sew in her accustomed way by piercing the material with an awl and passing the thread through the hole.

In her former life, Shanawdithit was used to a very different way of preparing food than on the stove at the Peyton's. As a Beothuk, she would have kindled open fires by striking two pieces of iron pyrites together close to a scrap of bird down or dried moss. During recent times the Beothuk had acquired a few European metal utensils, but they normally made their own pots and containers from folded birch or fir bark. The seams were stitched tightly with roots and were surprisingly watertight and durable. They were not placed directly over the flame, but meat could be stewed in them by keeping the water at boiling point through repeatedly adding heated rocks. The Beothuk also cooked meat by roasting it over the fire on long wooden spits. Bone marrow was a staple of their diet and caribou bones (up to 300 of them) were stored on posts around the mammateeks. They were cracked and boiled as needed, and the marrow made into a mush.

The Beothuk depended on dried foods, as did the Peyton household. Shawnadithit drew pictures of a Beothuk smokehouse with latticework shelves that allowed the air to circulate. Meat and fish were cut into thin strips, and when dried they would last a long time. These tasty snacks were light to carry and did not need further cooking, so this method of preservation was invaluable for their mobile way of life.

In contrast, the Peytons relied heavily on salted flesh, and on vegetables that could be stored in the root cellar. It was difficult to feed an animal once the growing season was over, so most of them were slaughtered in the fall. Poultry, eggs, and butter added variety. Wild game was also hunted and preserved, but flour, salt, sugar, tea, and other staples all had to be imported from Europe, and transported in ships from St John's.

The Beothuk had never seen salt, sugar, or butter, although they did clarify fat and store it in caribou or seal bladders. Shanawdithit had never tasted tea before she came to live at Sandy Point. Unlike the English, who relied on salted food during winter, the Beothuk put the hundreds of caribou carcasses from their annual fall slaughter into cold storage.

The meat was butchered and packed into birchbark boxes, which often weighed as much as 220 pounds. Once they were frozen and stored in pits, these packages would usually stay fresh for an entire winter. The eggs of seafowl were boiled, dried, and pulverized, and sprinkled onto broth. Eggs were also mixed with fat and liver, and stuffed into a seal's gut to make a kind of sausage similar to Scottish haggis.

Shanawdithit came into her own in the warmth of family life. Not able to converse with adults without great effort, Shanawdithit was deeply lonely. She transferred all her pent up emotions into love for the children, who adored her. When Bishop Inglis visited the household he was moved by the strong attachment between them, and said that the little ones would go to her more readily than to their own mother. After her death she was especially remembered for her love of children, and for her gentleness.

Shanawdithit could be feisty, too, and does not appear to have been at all cowed by Mrs. Peyton. Mrs. Gill, one of the other servants, loved to gossip and many years later vividly recalled a scene between Mrs. Peyton and Shanawdithit. Mrs. Gill said that Shanawdithit was often pert, and spoke back when Mrs. Peyton was cross with the servants. She would laugh in her face and say, "Well done Misses, I like to hear you jaw. That right," or "What de matter now, Miss Peyton, what you grumble 'bout?"

The Peyton household attracted many visitors, among them high-ranking naval personnel and clergy who were often piqued by the presence of a resident Red Indian. They would bring Shanawdithit gifts and she made every effort to accept the changes in her life. Another of the household servant's recalled how extraordinarily pleased Shanawdithit was with some fine clothes given to her by Captain Buchan, especially a pair of silk stockings and shoes. Captain Jones of the HMS *Orestes* also brought her clothes and Bishop Inglis noted how graceful she looked in them.

There were other visitors, too, from the neighbourhood. Shanawdithit became strongly attracted to a very shy fisherman who had bright red hair and a beard. One day she took the initiative to sit on his knee, which threw him into deep confusion. This was unusual behaviour for her. She normally displayed great modesty around men and reacted strongly if anyone tried to become too familiar. Shanawdithit told the family, through a mixture of mime and pidgin English, that her tribe was very strict in observing moral behaviour. She described how adulterers were burned alive at the stake, with the whole tribe solemnly dancing around the offender.

In any case, she was wary of English men in general, because she had been shot one day when her band was fired upon at Exploits. She showed the Peyton family areas on her palm and her leg where buckshot had left permanent scars. Mi'kmaq men terrified her, and Shanawdithit called them *shannoc* or "bad men." She particularly dreaded Mudty Noel (or Bad Noel Boss). Whenever he (or even his dog) came around, she ran screeching with terror to Mr. Peyton, and clung to him for protection. When the family wanted to know what had happened, she acted out a story from her past, crouching in terror and limping. Even now she feared that Mudty Noel would murder her and this dread was not entirely unfounded. Richard Routh wrote to Lord Hawkesbury in 1793 that the Beothuk were "shot at by the furriers and inhabitants with the same want of feeling that a deer or a bird would be killed."

In general, though, Shanawdithit enjoyed a peaceful family life while she lived at Sandy Point. Of all her skills the most appreciated by the family was her artistic talent. She kept the children constantly amused with her drawings and small models. They were fascinated by the enchanting tiny doilies she made for them by folding a scrap of birchbark and biting into it patterns of leaves, animals, and flowers. Shanawdithit also carved elegant combs from caribou horn for the family. Somehow she managed to convey what she wanted to say, although no one took the trouble to teach her English throughout the entire five years she lived there. As far as the outside world was concerned, it was noted that she was still alive and living at Sandy Point, but not much more thought was given to her. She lived an obscure existence out of the public eye.

Then William Eppes Cormack, famous for his trek across Newfoundland in search of the Beothuk in 1823, returned from abroad. It was 1827, and Shanawdithit had been living at Sandy Point for four years. Cormack, without delay, began to prepare for a second expedition into the interior. The Beothuk had not been seen in their usual haunts for several years, and furriers had moved in. Even in 1820 Buchan had noted at least 15 furrier's tilts close to where Nonosabusut was buried. A chance encounter with Judge Des Barres, though, put the enterprise on a different footing. The judge proposed creating a formal institution to promote public interest. Its first meeting took place on October 2, 1827, at the Twillingate Courthouse. A committee of prominent citizens was elected, and the new organization (to be named the "Boeothick Institution") was widely promoted at home and in Britain. John Peyton Jr. was not present at the meeting, but he was elected resident agent and corresponding member in his absence.

Cormack was facing impending bankruptcy, so he was relieved when he found his trip supported financially by the new institution. Fortuitously, he was able to engage three Native men who were used to wilderness travel. Cormack and his guides left from the mouth of the Exploits River on October 31, 1827, taking with them a Beothuk vocabulary of 300 words (perhaps compiled by the Reverend Leigh with the help of Demasduit), as well as shields to protect themselves from arrows.

After 10 days of extremely cold, snowy conditions, they reached Red Indian Lake. The entire area was deserted, and had such an eerie feel to it that two of the guides became extremely unsettled. When they came upon the Beothuk burial hut at Red Indian Lake, which contained the remains of Nonosabusut and Demasduit, Cormack was ecstatic. Here were many items of incalculable scientific interest. He proceeded, with no qualms, to desecrate the cemetery. He carried away numerous grave goods, including a small model of a birchbark canoe, the dress of the chief's infant daughter, two human figurines, and a wooden replica of a bird. But worse, he severed the skulls of Nonosabusut and Demasduit from their corpses and took them with him, too. His intention was to study them in a laboratory setting to determine racial origin and other physical data.

After 30 nerve-wracking days travelling a circuit of 300 kilometres through Red Indian territory, but still without sighting any Beothuk, Cormack's group arrived back at the English settlement on November 29. The trip had been so arduous that when Cormack called on the Peytons at Sandy Point, he appeared so gaunt and haggard that John Peyton Jr. did not immediately recognize him. On his return to St John's, Cormack again left for England, leaving his three Native guides to explore the north of Newfoundland, around the French fishing stations. The men returned on June 10, 1828, having travelled 800 kilometres. They had been promised a bonus of £100 if they discovered the whereabouts of the remaining Beothuk. Not only did they not get this, but also the Boeothick Institution was disappointed with the scouting party's performance and refused to hire them again.

All hopes were now pinned on Shanawdithit. It suddenly

seemed urgent to take control of her, make her a ward of the Institution, and transfer her from the remote outpost to St John's. John Peyton Jr. had not been present at the meeting when this plan was first proposed, nor had his consent been asked. It was assumed that the best thing for the committee might be to take the initiative and get the girl to St John's. In September 1828, two members of the Boeothick Institution, John Stark and Andrew Pearce, arrived at Sandy Point out of the blue. John Peyton Jr. was away at Stag Harbour Tickle, and Mrs Peyton was completely distraught. She did not want to give permission to let Shanawdithit go without her husband's knowledge, but they wore her down, and after three days she gave in.

Shanawdithit was immediately removed from the house and placed with the Reverend and Mrs. Chapman at Twillingate until her passage to St John's could be arranged. The Chapmans were concerned that Shanawdithit had no prior notice of the change and was given no time to prepare herself or say her goodbyes. She was, understandably, very upset and visibly agitated at being so forcefully separated from the only English friends and home she had ever experienced. Nevertheless, no one had thought it necessary to consult with her or give much thought to her feelings. The Chapmans, at least, went out of their way to be kind.

John Peyton Jr. was extremely angry when he found that Shanawdithit had been virtually kidnapped from his home in his absence. He was informed that since it was done through the Institution, of which he was a member, there could be no legal recourse, especially since he had never arranged formal custody. Cormack wrote to him defensively to say that he had intended to mention the transfer, but had delayed, and then when Peyton left on business, it was too late. Cormack's private jottings, however, put a rather different slant on the story:

> *Most fortunately with the assistance of two gentle-*
> *men similarly interested in the subject as myself I*
> *obtained the guardianship of the sole survivor ...*
> *she belongs to those who are most kindly to her, and*
> *now that she is among us here let us forget the past.*

Shanawdithit arrived in St John's on September 20, 1828. No one realized it then, but she had less than nine months to live. She was never very well after her return to St John's. It was a place of sad memories for her. The last time she had set foot in the garrison town she had been accompanied by her mother and sister, and had no idea of what the ensuing months would bring. People said that she seemed to find it a great effort even to smile, and that there was no feeling behind it. Shanawdithit was settled straight away into Cormack's middle-class bachelor household. She was disappointed and lonely, as she loved children and was used to the bustle of family living. Instead, she became an object of public display. Cormack put an ad in the local newspaper inviting anyone to visit his home that wished to meet Shanawdithit and the three Native guides who had travelled to the interior with him. It did not seem to occur to him that Shanawdithit might have felt frightened at being thrown into such close contact with people she had previously regarded as enemies.

Since she was very shabbily dressed for the wealthier homes of St John's, new clothes were quickly ordered for her. Cormack next ordered that a likeness be painted of her. He was scandalized that she had lived among English people for five years and had learned so little English. Only those who knew her well and were used to her attempts to communicate could understand her. He made it a priority to have her tutored in English, and found she learned commendably fast. She also now came into her own as an artist when Cormack began to supply her with paper and coloured pencils. With these tools, and her quick improvement in verbal communication, she was soon able to express herself clearly.

Cormack began to question Shanawdithit intensively, and whenever she talked about her people she broke down in tears. She recounted how they were all starving after being driven from the shores, and how her uncle and cousin had courageously begged help of the two furriers, only to be shot. Even at that time, she said, there were not more than a dozen Beothuk left, and certainly not enough to keep up the caribou fences that were essential to survival. Shanawdithit went over the Beothuk tribal history of the last years step-by-step with Cormack, illustrating their movements with minute and extraordinarily accurate detail. He was particularly interested in the scenes Shanawdithit had personally witnessed, especially Buchan's surprise arrival at Red Indian Lake, and the profound misunderstanding on both sides that had led to the marines being beheaded. She pinpointed the site where John Peyton Sr. had murdered a Beothuk woman on the Exploits River. She also added details about Demasduit's capture, which had not been known before, such as the death of her baby soon after the capture, and the murder of her husband's brother.

Besides this historical documentation, Shanawdithit made drawings of artifacts such as weapons, mammateeks, and clothing. Through her art she was able to depict the way they preserved food, as well as many other things of cultural significance. Cormack was particularly excited about Beothuk mythology, but unfortunately his notes on this were subsequently lost. Along with her drawings, Shanawdithit constructed small models of Beothuk canoes and sewed a full set of Beothuk clothing at Cormack's request. She also helped put together a rudimentary vocabulary of phrases like "don't be afraid," "not hurt you," and "we come to be friends," which would likely be of use in a hoped-for future encounter.

Cormack probably pressured Shanawdithit to produce an exhausting amount within a very short time (she was only with him about eight weeks). She may at times have felt rebellious, but one can only guess. On the back of one of her illustrations is a cryptic note in Cormack's handwriting. It says: "Nancy is a bad girl." Was Cormack insensitive enough to show her the grave goods and skulls he had stolen from the cemetery at Red Indian Lake? If he did, she must have felt deep shock. For her they were the cherished remains of beloved relatives. For Cormack, however, they were fascinating objects of great scientific interest. Most of them were later donated to Professor Jameson for the new Edinburgh University Museum. Nonosabusut's skull is still on view there as a curiosity.

Cormack was determined to eventually return Shanawdithit to her own people (if the opportunity arose) and simply could not understand why she was so terrified of the idea. She persistently refused to accompany him on proposed expeditions, trying to explain that, because she had lived with white people, she would be sacrificed to the *munes* (spirits) of Beothuk victims who had been slain by the whites or Mi'kmaq. He still didn't understand.

The scientist in him would have liked to take her to England with him to exhibit her before a number of scientific bodies. Circumstances prevented this when he finally became insolvent. Shanawdithit had arrived at his house in September 1828, and he was forced to leave for Britain in great haste in January 1829. In the late fall she was put under the care of Attorney General James Simms, who guaranteed to continue her education with ongoing lessons in the English language.

Cormack had achieved extraordinary success in collating an immense amount of material about the Beothuk in an astonishingly short time. Considering she was dying, Shanawdithit, too, achieved wonders in the way she co-operated with him.

In his humanitarian persona, his warmest memories of her were of her lively disposition, her strong sense of gratitude, and her great affection for her parents and friends. But, when appearing before the public, he merely referred to her in a detached manner as "this interesting female." And, when he left Newfoundland this time around, he was never to see her again.

Chapter 9
Shanawdithit Dies — A Stranger Among Strangers

A bitter November wind battled the rising surge of the grey Atlantic sea and swept in great gusts from the harbour up the steep hills of St John's. Shanawdithit shivered, and hugged her shawl closer around her shoulders. She coughed so much now that she rarely slept for long. It was difficult to keep going. She had so little energy that every step had to be willed.

This last change, so close to Christmas, had been almost too much to bear. Were the three Peyton children missing her at Upper Sandy Point? The little ones had grown very dear to her heart, and she to theirs. She had been part of their lives from the time they were born. Sadly thinking that she would not be there to share the gift giving and the rich food, she wondered whether they would understand why she had left. There had barely been time to say goodbye. She thought about the children a lot. The feasts at the outport were so different from her memories of her own tribal celebrations, and yet all her memories had an underlying joy and wonder for her.

At least she was among a large and boisterous family again, after the tense experience of Cormack's bachelor household. She silently practiced her new host's name ... Attorney General James Simms. He was a kind man, in spite of his important position. He was interested in her people's history and considerate of her welfare. She was grateful that he had hired a woman to take care of her needs. It was good to have someone with her when her panic, brought about by the exhausting bouts of coughing, came on. It was astonishing, too, to be living in such a wealthy household.

William Cormack's passage to England was booked for the end of January. He seemed to be in and out constantly, worried at leaving with so much still to be done. He crammed in visits to her at the Simms's house, but he was only one among many callers in their busy social life. He was pleasant, with his dry Scottish manner, but tiresome in the way that he was always intent on getting information from Shanawdithit.

Much as she had mixed feelings over his part in having her dragged away from the outport so dramatically, Shanawdithit knew that he desperately wanted to record her people's story before it was too late. He still looked gaunt and ill after his recent hazardous trip to Red Indian Lake. She had tried to co-operate, but he was a cold man, and only seemed to process things inside his mind. Perhaps if she gave him something more personal to remember her by it would soften his heart. She snipped off a lock of her hair and carefully braided it, then added two small rocks (a rounded piece of granite and one of quartz). The rocks she warmed for one last time between her palms, absorbing their energy. Treasured things, she knew, should be passed on. These two rocks embodied the feel and smell of her native home. Cormack received her gifts with his usual manner of scientific detachment. He was pleased she had given him some demonstrable proof of his commitment to her people's cause. He thought he might be able to weave the lock of hair into his stories and speeches. The rocks, however, were simply objects to him. When he got to England, he gave them to the Museum of the Mechanic's Institution as curiosities. Once there, they were catalogued and later lost.

Shanawdithit continued to struggle with her English lessons after Cormack sailed for Britain, but she became increasingly apathetic as her illness flared out of control. The tuberculosis filled her lungs, and the flow of mucous made it more and more difficult to breathe. At first she sat quietly by a window in her comfortable new home, sewing or working at crafts, while gazing out at the hills. Winter gave way to spring.

The time soon came, though, when Shanawdithit was too exhausted to leave her bed. Her bedroom was organized as a sick room. A sheet wrung out in carbolic acid was hung in the doorway to control the flow of germs into the main part of the house, and a folding screen shielded her from draughts. She was alternately tortured by thirst and drenched with sweat. Her hired nurse gently drizzled water on her dry lips, or swabbed her down with a refreshing mix of vinegar and water. The most painful aspect of her illness was her wracking cough. The nurse sat her up in bed and encouraged her to clear her chest of sputum. The poor young housemaid was kept on the run, burning the sodden rags in the stove and sterilizing all the utensils in the sickroom with a solution of bichloride. Mrs. Simms delivered cooling drinks for her fever, as well as fish and meat soups and custards to build up her strength. Dr. Carson was always near at hand, but there was little he could do beyond trying to ease her suffering.

Towards the end of May the disease suddenly worsened, and it became clear that she needed more care than the Simms could provide in their home. Dr. Carson and James Simms gently prepared her for a move to the hospital. Shanawdithit was warmly wrapped in blankets and carried down to the family's private carriage. She weakly raised her head for a last glimpse of the hills. So many years ago, after the great ships arrived, her ancestors had been driven from their heights. Drawing on a depth of spirit, which the weakness of her body could not overcome, she silently reclaimed her heritage in this place. She, alone as she was, still represented her race through her living presence, and in silent prayer she gave the future into the hands of the Great Spirit. Then, one last time, she surrendered to the white-skinned men. Shanawdithit was carried, not to a sacred sweat lodge in the heart of her community for physical and spiritual relief, but to isolation in a hospital.

Even though many people genuinely cared about her, she was still a stranger among strangers. The only white family she had grown close to, the Peytons, lived several days' journey away along the coast. Had anyone sent them word of her grave illness? She was always told so little. Besides, why would they come? She had only been their servant. A privileged one ... but still ... a servant.

She grieved about the absolute nature of her isolation, not only from all the people she had ever loved, but also from the spiritual world. One of her greatest fears since leaving Red Indian Lake had been that, when she died, her people would not be there to perform the sacred rites. Rites that would help her find the way back to her ancestors. None of these Christian people around her had the knowledge to cradle her weary bones in birchbark or offer sweet smoke for her journey. No one would re-anoint her body with grease and red ochre in the name of her tribe. No one would say proudly, "This woman is Beothuk." There were no grave goods to lay beside her to help her flourish in the afterlife (the rocks she had given to Cormack would have been her grave goods). The only representations of tribal life that she now had were models of canoes and other cultural objects that she had manufactured with her own hands to satisfy the curiosity of white people. Shanawdithit was deeply worried about the consequences of having lived among the enemy. To do so, under any circumstances, regardless of loss of choice, was to break the taboo laid upon her from birth. Would the spirits of the ancestors disinherit her? Would she become one of those lost souls condemned never to see the country of the good spirit, the country far away where the sun goes down behind the mountains? She yearned forgiveness.

Lying in her hospital bed, knowing that she was at the crossroad, she carefully went back over her actions throughout her years at Sandy Point. Yes, she had gone to church as she was bidden, and behaved with decorum, kneeling when others did, and paying respect to the solemnity of the occasion. But she had determinedly held fast to her own beliefs. Not once had she given her captors the satisfaction of believing that she had absorbed their faith. Quite the opposite. When Bishop Inglis visited her at the Peyton's, he complained that even after five years she knew so little of the Christian faith that he could not baptize or confirm her. As she drifted in and out of consciousness, she revisited those dreadful moments when she had returned alone from burying her mother and sister. She thought about how comforted she had been when she had taken off into the wilderness for days to be with their spirits. She had returned to the outport so uplifted that she sang and laughed and talked to herself. She had never allowed the taunting of the settlers to destroy that.

Now at this moment of her own death, peering into the shadows of the clinical ward, Shanawdithit was aware of the presence of spirits around her hard, narrow hospital bed. Suddenly, it was as if she had returned to the soft boughs lined with furs within her mammateek. She could smell the goodness of her homeland, of the earth and trees, of the fragrant smoke from offerings of sweet grass. The heat of a campfire seemed to warm her chilled body. As from a great distance, she could hear chanting, then, unmistakably, her Beothuk name was called ....

Shanawdithit died on June 6, 1829, and for convention's sake her names were combined on the burial certificate as "Nancy Shanadithi." She did not know her age when she was captured, since the tribe did not reckon in years, but she may have been as young as 17. Shanawdithit's body was laid in a coffin, as Demasduit's had been, but no attempt was made to return her home. Several obituaries were written on the occasion, but were more about the extinction of the tribe than about her death. Cormack, who had struggled so valiantly to record her memories, might have written something personal, shown some feeling of personal loss, but he didn't. He wrote, instead, with the detachment of a scientist examining an interesting and unique phenomenon. Dr. Carson, too, although he was deeply caring of both Demasduit and Shanawdithit during their illnesses, and had admired them both, also committed himself only to a scientific study of the Beothuk.

Shanawdithit had feared that she would not be given the traditional rites. But, in the end, it was even worse than that omission. Not only did Dr. Carson perform a post-mortem examination of her body, he severed her head and presented her skull to the Royal College of Physicians in London, England. He included with it a note that it exhibited certain peculiarities that warranted further study. Years later, in 1938, Shanawdithit's head was dispatched to the Royal College of Surgeons, where it was destroyed by a bomb in World War II. Meanwhile, what remained of her headless body was interred with a ceremony by the Reverend Frederic H. Carrington in the old Church of England graveyard on the south side of St John's Harbour. Did anyone think to bury any Native artifacts with her? It is not known. It is assumed, though not recorded, that she received the Christian rites at the last.

Shanawdithit's grave was lost when the railway was routed through the area in 1903. A plain stone cairn was later erected nearby. There are steps that lead up to a plaque, which reads:

This monument marks the site of the Parish Church of St Mary the Virgin during the period 1859 and 1963. Fishermen and sailors from many ports found a spiritual haven within its hallowed walls. Near this spot is the burying place of Nancy Shanawdithit, very probably the last of the Beothics, who died on June 6th 1829.

Epilogue

It seems that even this monument may now be in jeopardy. *The Globe and Mail* on Tuesday, July 29, 2003 writes fittingly and to the point: "The trouble with material evidence is its fragility. Take, for instance, the fate of Shanawdithit, the woman believed to be the last of the Beothuks. Construction of a new sewage-treatment plant is currently underway which will disturb Shanawdithit's memorial site and may disturb a graveyard believed to be her final resting place."

Shanawdithit's death and the realization that even if a remnant of the tribe might still remain in the wilds, the Beothuk had for all intents and purposes become extinct, generated a great deal of guilt. The Beothuk were idealized, and the settlers probably unfairly demonized. Some terrible acts were certainly committed, but by both sides. In recent years, a more positive and balanced understanding of the complexity of events has come about. Worldwide, the endless movement of peoples in search of food and land has often brought about widespread displacement and starvation. Whole populations were and still are affected by epidemics, climate fluctuations, and international warfare. The Beothuk people were casualties of all these factors, but, living on a small island, they had nowhere to run.

The great interest in Beothuk history and culture

generated in the last few decades resulted in the restoration of the Boeothick Institution, which had ceased to function after Shanawdithit's death. It was given the more modern name of Beothuk Institute and was opened on October 2, 1977, 170 years after its closure. The intention behind its revival was to encourage, through education, a better understanding of Beothuk culture as well as that of other Native peoples of Newfoundland.

Shortly after the Beothuk Institute re-opened, Gerry Squires, a Newfoundland artist, told the members of a remarkable vision of a Native woman that he had experienced at the Bay of Exploits. His story so moved those who heard him that the Beothuk Institute decided to erect a bronze statue of a Native woman to commemorate and honour the Beothuk people.

The figure symbolizes a momentous change in public attitude, from the stereotypical concept of the Beothuk as "semi-human savages" to the affirmation that the Beothuk were a people of profound human dignity, courage, and integrity. Their struggle to survive in the face of unimaginable loss and change is a heart-wrenching lesson in the tortured evolution of human history.

Further Reading

Crummy, Michael. 2001. *River Thieves*. Toronto: Anchor Canada.

Francis, Daniel. 1992. *The Imaginery Indian*. Vancouver: Arsenal Pulp Press.

Morison, Samuel Eliot. 1971. *The European Discovery of America*. The Northern Voyages A.D. 500–1600. New York: Oxford University Press.

Paul, Daniel, N., *We Were Not The Savages: A Mi'kmaq Perspective on the Collision Between European and Native American Civilizations* New Edition. Black Point: Fernwood Publishing, 2000

Reid, John G. 1987. *Six Crucial Decades. Times of Change in the History of the Maritimes*. Halifax: Nimbus Publishing Ltd.

Such, Peter. 1973. *Riverrun*. Toronto/Vancouver: Clarke, Irwin & Co.

Tuck, James A. 1976. *Newfoundland and Labrador Prehistory*. Ottawa: National Museum of Man.

Wright, Ronald. 1992. *Stolen Continents*. The "New World" Through Indian Eyes. Toronto: Penguin Books.

Useful Web sites abound. Some suggestions are:

Newfoundland and Labrador Heritage
http://www.heritage.nf.ca

Memorial University of Newfoundland
http://www.mun.ca

Provincial Museum of Newfoundland and Labrador
http://www.nfmuseum.com

City of St John's
http://www.stjohns.ca

St John's InfoNET Home Page
http://www.infonet.st-johns.nf.ca

Bibliography

Alexander, David. 1988. "Newfoundland's Traditional Economy and Development to 1934." *The Acadiensis Reader: Volume Two.* 11-33

Anon. 1903. *The Untrained Nurse.* Boston: Angel Guardian Press.

Brown, Stuart C. 1993. "Far Other Worlds and Other Seas: The Context of Claims for Pre-Columbian European Contact With North America." *Newfoundland Studies 9,* no. 2: 235-259.

Guy, John. 1957. *The New World. A Catalogue of an Exhibition of Books, Maps, Manuscripts and Documents, With Transcripts of five Unpublished Documents Relating to the Early History of the North American Continent.* London: Lambeth Palace Library.

Howley, J.P. 1915. *The Beothucks or Red Indians.* Cambridge: Cambridge University Press.

Marshall, Ingeborg. 1996. *A History and Ethnography of the Beothuk.* Montreal & Kingston, London, Ithaca: McGill-Queen's University Press.

Moore, Christopher. 1991. "Colonisation and Conflict: New France and Its Rivals (1600-1760)." *The Illustrated History of Canada*, ed. Craig Brown. 105-188 Toronto: Lester Publishing.

Moore, Lisa. Tuesday, July 29, 2003. "Mi'kmaq Paddy-whack: Skeletons in the Closet." The Globe and Mail, Page R1.

Pope, Peter E. 1993. "Scavengers and Caretakers: Beothuk/ European Settlement Dynamics in Seventeenth-Century Newfoundland." *Newfoundland Studies 9*, no. 2: 279-293

Ray, Arthur. 1991. "When Two Worlds Met" *The Illustrated History of Canada*, ed. Craig Brown. 17-104 Toronto: Lester Publishing.

Rowe, Frederick W. 1977. *Extinction: The Beothuks of Newfoundland.* Toronto: McGraw-Hill Ryerson.

Sack, R.D. 1986. *Human Territoriality, Its Theory and History.* Cambridge: Cambridge University Press.

Speck, Frank G. 1914. *Beothuk and Micmac.* Indian Notes and Monographs. New York: Museum of the American Indian, Heye Foundation, Misc. 3, no. 22.

Tuck, James A. 1993. "Archaeology at Ferryland, Newfoundland." *Newfoundland Studies 9*, no. 2: 294-310.

Upton, L.F.S. 1979. *Micmacs and Colonists. Indian-White Relations in the Maritimes 1713 – 1867.* Vancouver: University of British Columbia Press.

Acknowledgements

I am deeply indebted to many authors for their contribution towards what is known of the Beothuk. I have drawn especially on the meticulous research of James P. Howley, Ingeborg Marshall, Frederick W. Rowe, and James A. Tuck whose work collectively brings the pieces of myth, hearsay, and fact miraculously together.

Photo Credits

Cover: National Archives of Canada (C-038862) / Jennifer Stead. National Archives of Canada: pages 72 (C-092599), 95 (C-038862), 106 (C-038862).

About the Author

Barbara Whitby is a freelance writer in Halifax. She developed a life-long fascination with the Beothuk story after she emigrated to Canada from England in 1960. Now retired, she hikes, belly dances, acts as a film extra, and enjoys life as a great-grandmother. Through writing and the occasional radio broadcast, she shares an ardent interest in history, spirituality, healing, and travel.

OTHER AMAZING STORIES

These titles are available wherever you buy books. If you have trouble finding the book you want, call the Altitude order desk at **1-800-957-6888**, e-mail your request to: **orderdesk@altitudepublishing.com** or visit our Web site at **www.amazingstories.ca**

New **AMAZING STORIES** titles are published every month.